A Paean to Hunter

By: Seralita

Contents:

Introduction

Part one: Heartbreak
    A catalogue on Depop

Part two: Bile
    Interlude I
    Interlude II
    Interlude III

Part three: Beginnings
    A matter of yuanfen
    A correspondence

Part four: Love
    A reconciliation
    A retrospective

Acknowledgements

Introduction

A Paean to Hunter
He is both a hero and a villain, a true renaissance man, whom I love more than words could allow.

Seralita opened a Depop online shop called Havisham.Medea to make an exhibition of the wrongdoings of her on-again off-again partner Hunter who had once again abandoned her.

The listings of her designer-labelled apparel for sale vaulted her into transnational visibility, and the shop became the vehicle of a very public and occasionally dramatic chronicle of her relationship, which each listing of her items described at length in lieu of the actual items for sale.

This book presents an a-linear narrative through Seralita's chronicling of her memories and reflections on her relationship with Hunter. The relationship is simultaneously unique and mundane, certainly, it is turbulent. Seralita invites comments and correspondence with numerous women worldwide, and, ultimately, seeks a conversation with Hunter himself.

Havisham.Medea embodies Seralita's contrarian spirit. While the shop appears ostensibly as a medium for the public shaming of Hunter, and this book is presented as a parody of a paean, both the shop and book, are unmistakably a platform for the strong declaration of her unceasing love for her significant other.

Foreword

Asian woman driver; I lived up to the stereotype today when I entered a hard bend with a deliberate and urgent sharp swerve at a speed far greater than I should have maintained during the downpour. I realized by the jerk of the wheel from left to right under my grip, the sudden loss of tension and the incongruent traction, as I saw the steel posts sweeping up fast on my left and the tide of oncoming traffic on my right; I had lost steer control while still travelling at speed and was facing impending death.

It was deliberate, the choice to not brake before entering the turn. I made the decision on a whim. I remember the thought process clearly: why not. It wasn't because I really believed that I would make it. I wouldn't have made the turn at that speed under normal and dry conditions.

I applied the brake lightly while the car was in midturn, but by then it was already in drift and braking threw the car into tension. Electronics came alive urgently, flashing at me to deliver information that was already clear to me; the vehicle had lost stability and I had lost control.

There was no 'life flashes before your eyes' bullshit. I dunno, I could hear the beeping of the car's auto hazard indicator as it went off, see the flashing lights on the dash, and feel the sudden looseness of the vehicle as it began to drift. I knew that at any moment it could enter a spin that I had no control over. In those calm seconds it suddenly became very logical:

1) If the car carried me left, it would be totalled, I was about to die on impact with the steel posts.
2) If I was going to be borne right, it would be the same outcome but with more casualties.
3) I wondered if I would feel the impact at the moment of collision.
4) A flash of regret for my dog and my parents, if they were going to have to be the ones to ID me.
5) I chose to leave it to fate and not apply brakes or attempt to correct the spin.
6) I thought of Hunter and then I waited.

It was ironic because I had spent the day at a first aid training course. It was a more practical session than those that I had attended previously. The instructor played a clip of a drowned man being brought back to life with CPR. My mind drifted from the scene on the screen. I recalled the two separate points in my life when I had directly looked upon the death of close ones. In both cases, resuscitation was far beyond possible. The first time I was with Hunter. The second time I was alone in a room of people.

There had been foreshadowing only moments earlier in the day. Going 80 mph I had blitzed down a highway that was torched white with sleet rain and the floodlights of oncoming traffic. I had rolled the dice on that moment of blindness- because why not live or die when he's not here to draw a difference and distinction. At that moment I had closed my eyes. When I reopened them moments later, it was with a mixture of both relief and disappointment that I saw the road was still there ahead of me.

Is that the definition of impulsivity? Those decisions in the moment like a snapped nerve or a sudden jolt of electricity that bypasses the gatekeeper to making sound decisions. It builds like a roar that can't be contained and ultimately the decision is made to succumb to it, not out of futility, rather with a conscious desire for the anticipated self-effacement and a curiosity to know how that could be.

I remember my thoughts as I had approached the bend. I was traveling fast. The rain was coming down hard and forming pools across the road. It was dusk. I saw the bend as I approached it and I wasn't slowing. I was outside of myself and looking down at this person driving and nearing the turning point, and I remember wondering why wasn't she slowing? Yet I was also answering myself because it was clear to me: simply, why not.

Part one
Heartbreak

Seralita's Depop: Havisham.Medea

19th July 2020

Shop   Likes   Saved   Reviews

A catalogue of heartbreak

> **Active today**   > **0 Sold**

Bio: Breakup selling everything I wore/hardly worn stained with his memory his name is Hunter he's vividly despicable.

https://instagram.com/havisham.medea

0 followers
0 following

Each item carries a narrative that refuses to fade out of memory, festooned in nostalgia in the shade of antique rose as so often is the color of the fabric yet it fails to saturate the lens of retrospect.

> May each article of apparel carry
> forth to share the knowledge of his
> supreme ass-ness.

A catalogue on Depop

19th July 2020

Item 1:
Shrimps coat. Antique rose and black, excellent condition, worn only a handful of times, purchased for >$660, size UK 6 (xs) #shrimps.

Price A$400.00

21st July 2020

Depop Msg: Millaxxxx
Hi! You have lovely taste so had to grab this Shrimps jacket. Thank you!

19th July 2020

Item 2:
Shrimps shiny vinyl Hokus Coat with bubble-gum pink faux fur collar, size UK6 (xs).

The fur condition is perfect, some wear-induced change in texture at the inner elbow of the sleeves, otherwise in great condition. The vinyl material is lightweight, thin and shiny. Purging this from my wardrobe along with everything else as though it would exorcise his demonic presence that pervades every aspect of my life and sours every memory and notable association in geography and culture, essentially haunting all that I used to love by the nauseating spectre of his villainy.

The ass.

$10 shipping within Aus.

Price A$100.00 SOLD

22nd July 2020

Depop Msg: amyxxxx
Hi! Thanks so much!! Love the coat! ps you are an angel much unlike the despicable h*nter. Hope you're doing okay x

19th July 2020

Item 3:

Shrimps Hokus Coat! Size UK6, pink collar in great used condition, coffee stain on the inside pocket lining (not visible from the outside.

Price dropped not because I don't love this coat- I literally staked it out for months waiting for it to be released. It's just unbearable to wear it now without the association with him and I have to let it go, although I will unlikely ever let go of the bitterness and resentment that I feel towards him as his actions were galling.

$130 postage included if you promise to dm him the following on msger: #istandwithMargaret and #Hunteryouareanass

Price A$150.00 SOLD

31st July 2020

Depop Msg: helenxxxx
Ps I'm obsessed with all of your captions and I hope you are doing ok post breakup.

19th July 2020

Item 4:
Vetements reversible bomber jacket: size xs polyester outer shell, and wool inner shell.

Rare find, worn a few times, some wool piling. I fit a size UK6/FR34, the jacket fits true to size for an oversized look.

Price A$400.00 SOLD

28th July 2020

Depop Msg: honeyxxx
Hi hun! Just received the jacket thank you for sending so quickly! I promise to round house kick any men named Hunter whilst wearing this in your honor.

20th July 2020

Item 5:
Lonely Lingerie Winona bra, in amethyst with underwire. Size Aus 8B (30B in US). Worn once for my ex whom I now hate

infinitely. His name is Hunter, he's an asshole. The bra's condition is good as new.

Price A$30.00 SOLD

20th July 2020

Item 6:
Lonely Lingerie bra in black. Lacey in the boob area, velvet straps 3 eye hooks. As new, worn once.

Price A$30.00 SOLD

23rd July 2020

Depop Msg: biancaxxxxxxx
Hey lady! I'd like to buy both of your lonely bras, possible to do a bundle postage please? X
Also, I hope you're ok! I know the feeling; it can only go up from here.

20th July 2020

Item 7:
Crochet mini dress perfect for summer, really great condition, rayon material.

Thrifted from a store on Crown St, worn once to the beach.

We drove down south over Xmas 2018, to beaches along Wollongong and it was perfect we could have just died there, under the blaze of the summer sun, reclining in hotel rooms, car tripping down to falls, and through the bush.
It wasn't to be.

Size UK6.

Price A$25.00 SOLD

29th July 2020

Depop Msg: cliixx
Hi there! Super interested in this dress, would love to purchase. Just came across your page and am enjoying the heartbreak narrative attached to these items of clothing. Would just like to say heart goes out to you.

21st July 2020

Item 8:
Love Moschino shopper bag, large, brand new with tag, vegan leather. Price dropped as SUPER keen to be rid of this. For real. ASAP. Out of my sight.

Circa 2018? Cos that's when it was given to me by an ex-girlfriend.

We were super tight, but she leveraged my waning relationship with Hunter against me, in efforts to foster our own friendship, positioning herself as the defining feature that could preserve the relationship.

Later on several occasions when he and I broke down, she reached out to him in the guise of looking out for me, but really to manipulate him against me and here's the kicker- he believed her over me and prioritized her who did nothing for him except simple flattery through her actions, which definitely overstepped the boundaries- over me who gave up everything for him.

I let go of the both of them.

Their actions are purely disgusting.

Comes with a dust bag, label tag and card inside- can take a photo if required. Is in pristine condition, it makes me want to throw up.

Price A$80.00 SOLD

1st August 2020

Depop Msg: storyxxx
I'm glad that toxic friendship is over! no time for that are you happy with me going ahead and purchasing this? :)

1st August 2020

Reply: Seralita
Yes, please x and thank you for your support☐.

1st August 2020

Depop Msg: storyxxx
Done!

21st July 2020

Item 9:
Dr Natasha Cook Concentrated Moisturizer. 90% full, purchased in May this year.

I charged the cost to his card WHY??? Cos I put $$,$$$ into supporting his ass and he dropped me.
I used to care about skincare- even more so in my early 20s. When he and I met, I shared my moisturizer with him, it happened to be this label. I have sensitive skin; this never broke me out and kept my skin hydrated & even. He loved it too. So rather than using mine all the time, I just got him a couple of products. He was never self-conscious about using skincare. He even let me use the CC cream by the same label on him, I buffed it in as I would have done for myself. When he ran out, I mailed him extra product bc this isn't available (or wasn't at that time?) in the States.

I still love this range esp the cleanser!! It's the bomb-major. But I just don't want to look/use this right now.

Price A$40.00

21st July 2020

Item 10:
He gave this to me the first time that he left Australia and left me behind. He had thrifted them from another departing traveller. I didn't realize the symbolism at the time, and neither did he, obviously because neither of us read Chinese (him even less than me bc he's not Chinese), but the coasters represent a pair in perfect matrimonial union: the dragon and the Phoenix. The only way, he told me, that he could come back to Aus is if we were married.

He had already used up his working visa (all two years) working as a bartender. He had to leave to return home for USA or onwards to further travel. I never used these coasters. They've just stayed in my drawers. I don't know if I'm letting these go. Dm if you're keen, unlike the other items, don't hit buy on these straight up w/o msging please x I won't ever use these n can't bear to come across them when I'm rummaging thru my shit but just can't seem to let them go. They're part of the mythology of our relationship.

Price A$1000.00

21st July 2020

Item 11:
Alexander Wang mini skirt with silver metal balls along the hem. Marked size 0. It is true to size, I fit a XS/UK 6.

I wore this skirt to pick up takeaway from the Jap restaurant for him while he slept - it was the first time he passed me the keys to his bike and home. I didn't even know him, and at that point, I didn't even think I liked him, and I was surprised that he trusted me so completely. I thought that he was an innocent and I started to let him in from that point.

Price A$200.00

21st July 2020

Item 12:
Acne Studios oversized wool scarf in fuchsia.

Got this in 2018. Worn out on our first date, he took me to the Winery and then back to Low302 where he worked as a bartender. Also wore this with a Christopher Esber black mini dress and moto boots when he took me on his bike from his place in Redfern to Bondi. This scarf came out with me to the United States and then back. It's in great condition. I love it. He was embarrassed by how pink and eye-catching it was, it's quite oversized.

It's associated with our fonder memories.

Price A$350.00

21st July 2020

Item 13:
Shrimps pink knit size UK8, worn, slight change in wool at inner armpits, well maintained used condition. Please buy this I don't want to look at it and think about him.

Got this in 2016-2017-ish? I wore this label a lot while I was with him. It's not something I can return to or continue to see the same way with the same view of playfulness and vibrancy and lightness. It's all been tarred by him. Like a vat of spew, he's managed to soak into the material and ruin my appreciation of all the things that I used to love.

Price A$80.00 SOLD

1st August 2020

Item 14:
Shrimps frill neck knit, grey colorway in size xs (UK6). Well-loved but well maintained. I wore this label loads during my time in love with Hunter. If it wasn't so saturated with memories, I would hold onto it.

Hunter thought the word 'heaps' was odd usage, being American. He associated it as 'heaps of sugar' or heaps of sand, but not heaps as in 'lots' or 'loads.' He wouldn't say it was 'heaps good,' or that there were 'heaps of people.' Apparently, that was a distinctively Australian expression/usage of the word. He called everyone homeboy/homegirl. He was fond of making unique expressions and tbh they stuck. Like bumba. Bumba and bumbi.

There are conversations that I miss having with him.

Price A$90.00

18th October 2020

Depop Comment: _emmxx
You're heaps better off without Hunter babe xxxx

21st July 2020

Item 15:
Alexander Wang ball-chain bodycon pencil skirt with elasticated waist, size XS. Laser-cut feature down the side along the ball studs. Only worn once or twice.

Wore this label a lot when I was with him. I didn't think that he took much notice but at some point, he intuited the somewhat distinctive vibe as he mentioned in passing and pointed out that a later season item would suit my look.

I was surprised that he noticed but he was always v observant, just unexpected, I guess, and also flattering, it was a moment of fondness, and I always thought that he has a lot of steez unlike me in my funereal garb, occasionally interrupted by the odd dissonant splash of pink. Getting rid of this because it's painful to think about the fonder times with him.

Free postage within Aus.

Price A$60.00

21st July 2020

Item 16:
Sarah & Sebastian Pink Tiny Cluster Ring in Small. Featuring one white diamond and three pink sapphires, 9k yellow gold.

This ring came with me to USA when he asked me to go there for him. It came back with me when he changed his mind and decided he had no place for me after all in his heart when it no longer became convenient to him.

Price A$60.00 SOLD

23rd July 2020

Depop Msg: Jonesxxxx
Thanks so much for the speedy delivery, I hope you are recovering ok from your break up xx

21st July 2020

Item 17:
Vetements Bowie boots in size IT36. They are soo good Excellent condition. LOVE these. Worn car to carpet consistently. The one time I wore them out into the street was NYE 2018 when I was leaving Hunters to join him at his work Low302 where he was on shift for the transition. Haven't worn these since.

We spent NYE together and watched the fireworks from the top of the building. Aref let us and the two other couples remaining in the bar at that time, up the lift and onto the rooftop where we watched the clock drop, and it was the best NYE of my experience, and I was in love and he with me, as he held me, and we watched as the fireworks went off over the harbor.

I hate him and I loved him. If we change the tense it would be 'odi et amo.' And I would change the tense because as much as I hate hate hate him for his actions, I still very much love him.

Ready to let go now.

Price A$1400.00

1st August 2020

Item 18:
Shrimps mini embroidered playsuit in size UK6. It's cute, it's pink.

Clearly, I have a thing for pink as much as I am reluctant to admit this, the color appears to be a frequent trend in my wardrobe. When I moved to Petersham and started decorating my new place, I was instagramming for ideas to style my interior and came across an image of a kitchen with a mishmash of vintage and modern appliances and homewares, but with distinct color pops and occasional splashes of pink peeping through the overall. So, in that vein, I set about decorating my place. It ended up being blaring pink to the point that my housemate, a major sweetheart who lived at the front of the house- we had separate entranceways- came over and commented on the apparent obsession with the color theme.

I wore it to the beach with Hunter. I'm keen on it out of my sight.

Free post.

Price A$50.00

25th July 2020

Depop Msg: rapxxxxxxxxxxxxx
Hi there thank you for your order I've actually been looking at all your lovely shrimps items and wanted to say hope you are okay and fuck Hunter!

25th July 2020

Reply: Seralita
Thanks so much for your support !! I have a whole bunch of stuff assoc w Hunter to get rid of, just haven't had the time to really post but will get around to it this weekend. He was a real ass. Now he's an ass in the field take care lovely x

1st August 2020

Item 19:
Pleasure State Couture soft cup bra and panties set in purple lace with a diamanté hardware feature. Got this when I was a dancer years and years back, but never worn bc they looked too pretty. Now I don't have the occasion for them as I'm limiting myself to a life as a recluse a la Dickensian Havisham.

Price A$20.00 SOLD

1st August 2020

Item 20:
Allude cashmere sweater in red. Super soft 100% cashmere. Worn gently. Size XS.

I wore this when I was out and about making calls to him in the early mornings, every day, (PM for him in Boston due to the time difference). It was autumn here and getting on in briskness, and a particularly cold spring there, thick snow. This was one of the last purchases I made that year, with the idea to save for him while he was getting back on his feet following a motorcycle injury, and then subsequent events of significant trauma in his family.

I used to look forward to hearing from him daily, briefly or for hours. Now I can't bear to look at this.
Price A$150.00

1st August 2020

Item 21:
Dress Up wool-blend turtleneck crop. Size Aus 6. I got this from INCU. Dunno why I bought so many clothes from INCU. Ready to let this go.

It doesn't have history related to Hunter. I was dating (I used this term loosely) a delightful guy (not Hunter). He told me that I was really tight and should go purchase a practice device to stretch it out for him, among other pearls of wisdom.

Hunter was worse. Wasn't it Euripides who said that a wicked man who is also eloquent seems the most guilty of them all? He'll cut your throat as bold as brass because he can dress up murder in handsome words. He took everything from me and turned it around and said he never wanted it all. Then give it back. But he won't. He's a monster. My youth and what remains of my heart has been torpedoed by him and his villainy. How dare he turn it back around on me. To think that I dressed up for him, left behind home and country for him, turned aside all that was known and safe to be by his side.

Price A$30.00

1st August 2020

Item 22:
Rollas crop sweater top in XS from prob 2012/2013. I wore this out quite often when I was with him. He was into cropped tops. In fact, he was quite particular about fashion, being put together. Occasionally I worried whether I embarrassed him with my fashion sense (distinctly quite different from his in that I can be quite maximalist with color and texture). I think he liked it better when I was more pared down and wearing more muted and earthy colors.

This was a top I would wear often. If it wasn't for him, I would keep it as part of my collection as it's so well made and has great versatility and pairs with everything. Letting it go along with his intolerable bullshit.

Price A$35.00

1st August 2020

Item 23:
The Strokes open side cut off shirt. Perfect for beach/summer life. I thrifted this when I was working as an acupuncturist up in Proserpine/Airlie beach. This is definitely years pre-Hunter, but he has this thing for cut off shirts, he would remake t-shirts into cut-offs by taking to them with a pair of scissors and opening up the sides.

He made several for me, cut-offs and crops. This shirt pre-dates him and his actions, but I can't see it and not think of him.

Price A$25.00

1st August 2020

Item 24:
Acne western boots in size 36. These were a regretful buy. Got them for the narrow pointy toe witch vibe but didn't really get much wear out of them. What DID get Loads of wear was my patience and love when he time and time again broke both. The major ass.

Price A$90.00

1st August 2020

Item 25:
Jonathan Aston London pin-up stay-ups. Got this in 2009-10 when I was a dancer but never got around to wearing this pair to the pole.

Once Hunter sought my opinion as an ex-dancer, whether he could do something similar topless bartending or similar, like his housemate at the time was working as an established male model.

Hunter has an incredible rig- he works hard for it at the gym. He got it out often. But I told not to go for that option. Unlike his housemate, I told him, he had a softer heart. The industry would not suit him or be good for someone like him. For instance, myself, it hardened me and my opinion of all men. While seemingly innocuous by an external veneer of Asian-cute supplicant mildness, I was in truth more capable of closing my heart and acting out the jagged necessities that I knew were outside of the realms of his kinder and gentler imagination. And I told him he should keep this purity.

I loved him.

Brand new in packaging.

Price A$15.00

1st August 2020

Item 26:
APC white silk dress with ink spot pattern. Size xs from approx 2011-2012. Worn over, spent with friends who are no more, in times that have long passed, chapters long closed.

Price A$15.00 SOLD

2nd August 2020

Depop Msg: Emmaxxxxxxxxxxxx
Thank you! Really enjoyed reading your stories on each of your items, good riddance to him!

1st August 2020

Item 27:
Arnsdorf by Jade Sarita Arnott.

Translucent ephemeral white dress summer dress. Size UK6. Top is pale ecru silk and bottom half is pure white cotton, really delicate young and feminine, nostalgic and even more so in relation to the better times of when I wore them, once into the ocean. But I'm far from the Pacific now and far from those times.

Price A$25.00

1st August 2020

Item 28:
Purple summer dress. Thrifted, loose on me, best fit size 8-10, I'm UK6. Weighty satin with stretch.

Purple is a royal color. Neither he nor I come from royalty. He's from USA, ethnic background Italian-Swedish, I'm Chinese. Of note in my lineage, my third great uncle Xu Te Li who was the personal tutor to the polemical political figure Chairman Mao.

Hunter's family's spread across USA but they came together as one and it was clear that despite the distance they had so much warmth. It was apparent in their grief, the reason they gathered in late June 2019, and the reason that he asked me to fly to be with him. This color, in particular, something in its distinctiveness, makes me think of that strange time steeped in sadness but also a time of marvel as I was welcomed into their midst despite an outsider.

Maybe it's his mother, whom I just love, or his father who carries an incredible air and served in the Marines. It feels very royal.

Price A$20.00

1st August 2020

Depop Msg: sk4xxxx
Hey! Do you ship internationally? Also sorry about Hunter. Fuck that guy.

I get paid tomorrow, so I'll order this and perhaps a few other things. I'm a little obsessed with your wardrobe.

1st August 2020

Item 29:
Nodress the Label yellow velvet cheongsam. I liked the label; he seconded the buy. It's brand new without tag. Size is labeled S. Would best fit a size 8 for the body con look I think it's slightly loose on me.

The label is up and coming, by CSM student LuQi Yu. The dress came out in a collab with Opening Ceremony in 2017/2018 I can't remember - info can be googled.

I can't look at this dress and not think of him. I was originally very enthused about this label and was surprised that for once he and I were in agreeance - love this dress. Both the label/dress I can't see without thinking of him. Which reminds me, he was iffy on my sense of style, I remember showing him a set of Ashley Williams clips only to be knocked back. They said witch he said to the effect that I was a bitch.

I strongly decline to keep this dress.

Price A$90.00 SOLD

1st August 2020

Item 30:

Louis Vuitton vintage patent leather mini slip bag in a unique pale gold colorway with the monogram and gold hardware.

Authentic there's a serial number on the inside CA0939- ask for pics. The bag is well-loved n a unique piece w plenty of life x

I didn't wear this with Hunter, or anything ostentatiously major of designer house during that period tbh as I wasn't sure how comfortable he was, whether he would judge me or feel self-conscious. I wanted us to be as one in mentality, a family, and to share the same security I feel with him, a sense of stability that I felt he never grew up with or had experienced comfortably. He gave me a bottomless sack of darkness in return.

$220 free postage within Aus.

Price A$220.00

1st August 2020

Item 31:
<Screenshot of a section from Carson, A. Eros the Bittersweet>
GONE

All our desires are contradictory, like the desire for food. I want the person I love to love me. If he is, however totally devoted to me he does not exist any longer and I cease to love him. As long as he is not totally devoted to me, he does not love me enough. Hunger and repletion. (1977, 364)

Emily Dickinson puts the case more pertly in "I Had Been Hungry":

So I found
That hunger was a way
Of persons outside the windows
That entering takes away

Carson, A. (1986). Eros the Bittersweet: An Essay. Princeton, New Jersey; Guildford, Surrey: Princeton University Press. doi:10.2307/j.ctt7zv117

Price A$2122018.00

                                                       1st August 2020
Item 32:
Sarah and Sebastian one half of the half sun ring set. It's super fine and delicate in 9k yellow gold, I think. Size small.

The other half was lost in USA. Along with everything that I had given up my life for at the cost of everything that was known and stable for me, simply because he asked. It was a mistake and it cost me. I don't want to hold on to the other side of that set now.

It's just the ring :(I don't have any tag/box or proof of the label :(but it is legit and yea it'll just have to be my word, I got it from INCU like years way back- clearly had a thing with shopping at Incu I realize that it's where I got loads of the items I'm trying to offload now.

Price A$30.00 SOLD

                                                       2nd August 2020
Item 33:
Ellery Louis XVI bibbed silk dress in ecru. A really delicate silk shirt dress with lovely neck detailing. Super early days Ellery dress! Size UK8/US4/AU8.

Condition: great preowned condition, some light pulls close to the inner armpit and down the back seam and button holes, but nothing major and doesn't require repair or stitches, in my opinion.

The back is quite sheer, I wore this to a girl's bday not realizing that it's a bit transparent from the back as it's a light color. I think I only wore a black bra and g-string combo underneath n got stares all night not realizing the bare situation. Hence this dress became affectionately known as the naked dress. Definitely predates Hunter, letting it go cos it doesn't get much wear.

Price A$15.00 SOLD

                                                       2nd August 2020
Item 34:

Moschino vintage cropped sweater top with structured gold thread. Superb well-maintained condition. Really Love this top It's labeled IT40/US6/UK10 but it fits true on me I'm a size UK6. Cropped, midriff-bearing on someone taller than 5'4 - reaches just over my navel on me.

Again, I'm not keen on crop tops. Hunter has ruined that whole style for me, and this was something I wore heavily when I was with him. Moving on. He wanted to move on. This needs to move on. I'll hold onto the unrelenting bitterness though. That ain't budging.

Price A$60.00 SOLD

3rd August 2020

Item 35:
Alexander Wang Kori boots size 36 rose gold. Reluctant to let these go as they're very versatile and easy for everyday wear. They're in good condition.

I wore these when I went to Dana Farber, Harvard in Boston with Hunter to meet with a Professor. It was an exhilarating moment, showing up out of the blue due to the collision of circumstances that had brought me to USA, to meet him in person. I was so grateful to have Hunter there with me, his support, by my side it felt so right. We fought on the train back; I don't even remember what about. I regret it.

I remember how heated he became and I too in response became upset to the point of tears. I remember that it got to our stop and he just abruptly got off and left me to follow him. I couldn't understand why it had escalated so quickly so extremely, and I walked away from him after we left the platform. It was an uncomfortable car ride when his brother and sister-in-law picked us up. I remember ignoring him, avoiding his gaze whilst crying.

Free post.

Price A$150.00 SOLD

3rd August 2020

Item 36:

Alexander Wang Gabi boots in size IT/EU36, rose gold hardware. Literally worn once. Purchased 2-3 years ago but stayed in the box and are in excellent condition. I have too many iterations of the same boot. Letting these due to the memories associated with that aforementioned ex-non-romantic-girl-friend who danced on the lifeline of my relationship with Hunter, particularly as the thread started to fray.

Price A$650.00

3rd August 2020

Item 37:
Proenza Schouler mirrored heel boots size 36. Worn 2 times. Love these shoes a bit too much that I don't actually wear them which is a bit of a fail :s These didn't even get worn when I was with Hunter, I was kinda precious with them to the point where they got shunted to the back of my shoe storage and where they were left out of sight and out of mind. Letting go of this style of boot- I have repeats of this style (see other boot posts) it's ridiculous.

Price A$450.00 (no longer for sale)

3rd August 2020

Item 38:
Acne Studios pistol boots in size IT36 (they fit true to size I think because I'm standard IT36/UK3 in shoes). Very good condition has been re-soled and heel tips have been replaced once. You may be asking, Margaret, why have you got several pairs of what appears to be the same iteration of ankle boot. They're the perfect height and I can pretty much wear them all day without being trapped in the 9th circle of foot-hell by nightfall. Not related to Hunter. They were my favorite style of boots but it's time to move on from this shape and style. x

Price A$200.00 (no longer for sale)

3rd August 2020

Item 39:
American Apparel Breton/nautical stripes dress from 2009. One size fits all- has pockets !!! Dearly loved and ready to depart particularly as I'm getting on in my old age. Pre-Hunter era I remember that there was a different guy who was

so oh so troubling at the time, Ray, he used to work at American apparel, I broke up with my best friend at the time over an incident in relation to his lame ass- he's probably a lovely person now- goodness- but it was the end of an era my best friend and I were like Jane and Daria. Oh alas. He ensconced and absconded.

Price A$20.00

3rd August 2020

Item 40:
American Apparel lace stretch mini dress in faded ecru. Size XS/S. I'm a size UK6 and 5'4- it fits me as body con.

Fading and waning like a thousand suns imploding into nothing leaving behind only stardust so the O Gloria of my youth departs from me and in my old age this dress needs to retire from me onwards to caress skin that has yet to be kissed by betrayal and bitterness stained with the indelible splashes of heartache that like spots on the hands of the Lady refuse to out. From parties and gigs atop Kawa on Crown before it was 'dozed into its gentrified enclave, never touched the dancers' pole but stripped off time and time over to never be worn again, like so many pieces of lingerie that he claimed I never put on for him but in reality he just never noticed, of the seemingly endless that escaped his consideration, to be replaced by the more sensible O Bridget.

Didn't have trouble noticing others tho did he.

Price A$20.00

3rd August 2020

Item 41:
Vivienne Westwood Roman 3 strap sandals in size UK3 (I'm a standard Eu/IT36 in shoes) and fit true for me. Purchased in 2014.

These are dearly loved- have been well-maintained & resoled once to prolong longevity. Still got plenty of life and loads of mileage on the resole. Very good used condition.

Selling these, albeit reluctantly, but they mark a time that I would rather put behind. I wore them Loads when I was friends with a girl- the very same toxic friendship that I terminated as my relationship with Hunter ended. She attempted to leverage my desire for intimacy with him through her continuing 'friendship' with him as a way to manufacture a relationship with me in order to persuade me to assist her, as one of the many cronies that she pulled the strings on, all the while insisting that she had NO attachment to him and would choose me over him in an instant- after all, SHE neither loves nor cares for him in actuality.

She betrayed this statement obviously.

Price A$600.00

3rd August 2020

Item 42:
Acne Studios telde boots in bubble pink/black. Very lightly worn with some minor black marks on exterior shown in pics that would come off with a suede brush/eraser, overall really good condition. AW16 Size 36 EU/IT.

These are from a time when things were flush with pink. That time has passed. Currently, it is aggressively not-pink.

Price A$100.00   SOLD

5th August 2020

Depop Msg: Leanne Xxxxxx
Hi lovely, I just want to ask are you ok? I'm concerned for your welfare, your descriptions for your sale items are not actually about the items but about your life and emotions. If you need to reach out for help, please feel free to message me xxx

5th August 2020

Reply: Seralita
Hey there! thank you so much for reaching out and taking the time to look through my shop and my writing. I started this shop as a way to get a return out of the loads of clothes that I no longer wear, mostly due to their memory association, but also some vintage stock that I have building up in my closet.

It was a bad breakup, and in some ways this process of documenting random moments of his and my time together has been therapeutic, allowing me to memorialize those details that would otherwise be lost forever to time, and also to share the narrative/mythology of our relationship.

I don't want to hang onto some particular items for sure, and there are def some harsher moments, and I definitely hold recriminations against him. But I also still love him very much, though this may not be overtly apparent by the trend of descriptions I've been posting. Just yea in terms of the clothes- hope they can keep living on and continue to be loved even if yea not nurtured thru his and my relationship xx Anyway, thank you again for your support xxx I hope you have a lovely day.

5th August 2020

Item 43:
Lover silk midi skirt in soft ecru. A very delicate skirt, some light pulls at the seams that have been gently reinforced, overall good condition and a classic style Got it from INCU about 2012-2013.

Wore this into the ocean and out on summer days with him. It's time to let it go. It's a lovely skirt, but yea, just not going to get any more rotation of wear from me. I don't want to see it and think of him.

Price A$20.00 SOLD

5th August 2020

Depop Msg: Laura Xxxxx
Hey, what's the length of the skirt? I love your depop btw you've given me so many laughs over the last week. Clearly the better half of the former couple.

10th August 2020

Item 44:
Glow Recipe watermelon glow pink juice moisturizer. 2/3full, clean pump dispenser (60ml full-size).

Purchased Feb20 $62 Incl: 1/4 jar full-size sleeping mask (used the spatula & cleaned every time- I'm particular).

It smells amazing, is light & hydrating like spreading a gel of pink summer across your face. I also got the original sleeping mask & there was one time my housemate was super sunburnt & then super annoyed when I insisted on smearing the mask over his flushed face as I was convinced that the divine watermelon extracts would take away the bite of the burn. I'm not sure whether it worked he ended up buying a huge bag of ice which he took fragments from &proceeded to apply to his skin.

I don't find myself using much moisturizer these days. I suspect that is why the winter face situation is reaching a dangerously critical level of horrendous. Aging most rapidly particularly as I am about to depart my 20s yet still have not updated my skincare routine to reflect the drastic turn of the tide.

Price A$15.00 SOLD

10th August 2020

Depop Msg: Gemma X
Hey, I felt compelled to message u after going thru all your descriptions. I hope your broken heart is healing <3 I know it will, but only with time. But I see you're in good care w Eros the Bittersweet, and Simone Weil, and Emily Dickinson. Legit your words made my day, and you are a genius. So onwards <3 They didn't deserve you, they couldn't grasp your totality.

11th August 2020

Depop Msg: Scintalla:
This is an odd message, but I love the vulnerability in your descriptions when you talk about Hunter and your past (relationships). Sending you love and healing.

11th August 2020

Reply: Seralita
IBID (mostly)

11th August 2020

Depop Msg: Scintalla:
It's definitely apparent you hold a lot of love for him! Being 21, I recently understood that someone you care about can hurt

you over and over but you'll still love them and remember them till the end of time, strangely enough. It's really touching to see something raw on this site and it affirms how I felt (feel?) about somebody in my life and I suppose I felt more understood and connected when I read your thoughtful, poignant paragraphs. I'm rambling now lol but just wanted to thank you for that and for sharing it with the rest of us. Thank you for the love.

11th August 2020

Reply: Seralita
Thank you for sharing this with me x I appreciate it for sure it really sucks going through it, even at 29 ;) and no number of platitudes 'oh in time and with perspective' will change that reality. I don't like to think of this as a lesson-rather as each person that we come across we are blessed to share the chance encounter in time and space out of the billions of possibilities x I hope you are able to find peace n joy n love.

11th August 2020

Item 45:
Delicate filigree rings (two rings) from that shop in Surry Hills Somedays- I can't remember what brand they are got them years ago when that whole super fine jewellery look was kicking off. They are gold plated copper or bronze, I can't remember, but they don't turn green. The 3x gold coin ring is resizeable should be size M, while the pink enamel dot ring is not resizable size M in both rings. Letting them go because they don't go with how I dress now. They came with me to the US and back. I wore them on our earlier dates, and I remember taking off my jewelry n putting them on his nightstand when I treated him for his shoulder pain and back pain. He had his pieces too, a particular taste that was kind of clashing but somehow, he made it all work. He was unique in that way how he made it all work. Except for our relationship. He let that break. I gave him my engagement ring (a ring I had cast for myself) to safe keep. I had charmed it to contain a piece of my heart. He needs to return it.

Price A$20.00 SOLD

11th August 2020

Depop Msg: Bianca X
hey, I saw one of your posts and was intrigued by the caption (I think the watermelon glow recipe one) so I read the rest of the captions n they were a beautiful mix of hilarious n nostalgic n sad. Idk you n this won't mean much but I hope you find inner peace within eventually x all love.

I'm glad this can be a platform to help you commemorate what you had and come to terms with any emotional complexities xx

11th August 2020

Item 46:
Vintage United colors of Benetton wool-blend top in very good condition. Wore this heavily in 2008-2009 it's marked size M but can fit 6-10, just more fitted for size 10. It's not cropped length, just that 90s sits on the top of your hips length. This one is unrelated to Hunter. I'm going through my clothes storage. I wore this heavily at art school (COFA, now rebranded into the delightfully catchy UNSWAD).

Price A$70.00 SOLD

11th August 2020

Item 47:
This bracelet was a gift, real pearls, diamanté, and fish beading with an inscription that reads Joy, made with love. It was supposedly picked up on some various travels in the Philippines. I kept it untouched in my drawer. It's from an ex -not Hunter- who went volunteering-cum-culture shopping in South East Asia and picked this up for me supposedly.
I don't like it, I don't like him, perhaps someone else likes it?? Or likes him.

Price A$25.00

11th August 2020

Item 48:
Williwear denim jacket in size L in men. By Willi Smith, the designer who introduced streetwear to the catwalk. He invented streetwear, was the most high-profile black fashion designer of the 80s and influenced a generation, yet fashion history has largely forgotten Willi Smith.

>https://hypebeast.com/2020/7/willi-smith-williwear-black-fashion-designer-history
>https://www.theguardian.com/fashion/2020/jun/08/willi-smith-williwear-african-american-streetwear-catwalk

I thrifted this out of one of my exes' wardrobes, he never wore it and so I ensconced upon the item and kept it when we broke up. It fits as super oversized on me, but I like the look. It fit true to style on him. Vintage 80s, with design-intended fabric distressing at front and sleeve (pictured) very good condition.

Price A$100.00

11th August 2020

Item 49:
Williwear vintage men's denim vest in L 100% cotton (I'm UK6 160cm). Condition is v good but for the yellow stain at the inner collar (not noticeable when worn) was there when I thrifted it from the same ex's closet (not Hunter). Sure, it's intended for men but I wear it as a layering piece over 2 oversized sweaters that I also layer over skinny jeans n moto boots -a multi-tiered layered look that I imagine he would grimace to consider. Like how he would react to my Neuw sweater, which is no longer new as it increases in slub, yet never loses slouch- also a men's L n in a nondescript colorway. But it's perfect and I don't know why he was so resistant to wearing sweaters, perhaps it's too preppy and a phase that he grew out of back in high school- so it was always sweatshirts and cutoffs and mesh. I wish I had kept the one in ecru instead I'll just have to moulder in the few remnants that I clutch to tightly n continue to collect items that bear reminiscent qualities and be encased in time.

Price A$100.00

11th August 2020

Item 50:
Repetto Panam pump in shiny black patent. FR37. These shoes are really pretty and feminine as per the aesthetic of this French label as seen worn by various entertainers in the public eye such as Alexa Chung, Kate Moss, Lily Rose-Depp etc.

It's time to stop pretending that this pretty aesthetic suits me. The time for that flush of youthful optimism most appropriate to the ingénue has long passed, accompanied by my desire to continue to wear this pair of shoes. I got this pair in 2011 or 2012 but rarely worn, I think only on two occasions so it's in really good condition as it's just lived in the box it came in.

Price A$90.00

11th August 2020

Item 51:
Vintage corset?
Eye hook holes up the back, fits me size UK6 and A to B cup (I'm an A cup, but there is room for extra boobage). Black n form-fitting with some underwire-structure- boning down the front and sides, padded bra.

This was thrifted, worn during my time as a dancer. It's a great close fit. Hunter knew that I used to be a dancer, bc I told him. All the girls had to take stage names; we were told at the audition. Some girls made the cut, some were told they were probably not suitable for what was required in the role. Those that made the cut were given a subcontractor form to fill in n among the details was What is your stage name? I was kinda put on the spot, one of the girls (real name Claire) went for Clara (not a far stretch). For some reason that 90s anime Sailormoon came to mind, n I settled on Lita (Sailor Jupiter, soldier of love and courage). I initially thought about adopting Serena. Seralita is an amalgam of both.

This was one of my costumes the corset?top, not the stretch corduroy leggings in ecru.

Role requirements incl podium, private and shower shows where there was an expectation for 100% starkness and open legwork (min last 5mins per 15min show). Temperatures were toasty- strictly no touching. Not much different these days acc to Eden.

It's something that stays with you, why I told him to not venture into this industry even though Leigh was promoting his exploits as something glamorous he was into BDSM on the side n regaled Hunter with stories of how he left bruises on one girl n fucked her for like hour/s whilst taking a blue chew- which sounds incredibly unpleasant- but hey it's boys telling stories to boys to exercise the exponential potential for expansion of ego- anything goes I suppose. The story came up I think cos I was super loud when I was with Hunter, apparently, Leigh who lived on the other side of the house, n on the ground floor asked him who was the screaming chick. Jesus. Hunter was curious about Leigh's purportedly many and various exploits n asked me about my experience in the industry, n asked my opinion on whether he could do something similar, as Leigh kept suggesting, topless bartending, strip shows, bc he has a great rig n is cute.

But male n female strippers live in different worlds. I told him that his heart is softer than Leigh's. The experience hardens you and your outlook. I told him to protect his purity. I never saw people in particular men the same way.

#ilovedhim#lovehim#love#him#8

Price A$10.00 SOLD

11th August 2020

Item 52:
Vintage Adidas mini skirt, has light white paint marks on the back that don't detract and by happy accident match the existing white triple stripe label pattern.

This is from my storage closet. I haven't worn this in several years. Not fond of this label anymore because he wore it loads. In fact, when he broke his foot and had to emergency travel back to his brothers' in DC where it was snowing down heavily that year (Winter) I went around Sydney CBD and shopped a load of Adidas sweatshirts and the like for him cos I was worried that he only had summer clothes on him and would be super cold and couldn't shop from his brother's on his broken foot and his limited working holiday traveller's savings while unable to work for the time being- so I got a bunch of Adidas stuff for him Not enthused about Adidas or athleisure myself tbh.

Size XS.

Price A$10.00 SOLD

11th August 2020

Item 53:
This jacket reminds me of his Ferrari jacket- his jacket was XL.

There's an incredible story attached to how it came into his possession Aref at Low302 had a regular who I think was a bookie n kept a long tab that grew so long he eventually ran out of options on squaring up. One day he came into the bar and just left Aref his incredible condition Ferrari racing jacket apparently valued at $$$$$'s and that was that.

Beautiful Mel, Aref's girl who managed there was wearing it one time – she's tiny n gorgeous n the jacket just swamped her but in the most incredibly flattering way- and Hunter was super enthused about the jacket- so much so that Aref asked him if he wanted it- n swept it off Mel's shoulders n just straight up gave it to Hunter there n then. She was furious. Hunter was ecstatic. N that's how he came into possession of the XL one of a kind authentic Ferrari winners' jacket from the 90s.

At least that's how I remember him telling the story to me. It's in DC now.

Price A$2122018.00

11th August 2020

Item 54:
Sandler vegan leather bucket bag. This is also unrelated to Hunter and were a random gift from a different ex. He would get me a random surprise present every week. This is one of them. I can't remember what I got him, but every once in a while, I would surprise him too. We ended up breaking up bc I wasn't in love with him; one day it just became apparent as the very scent of him was suddenly repugnant to me, and so shortly afterwards I ended it. I broke up with him before Valentine's Day, bc I didn't want him to go to immense effort only for the relationship to go south immediately afterwards.

There were very strong reasons for why we could not work it out.

Price A$25.00

11th August 2020

Item 55:
Thrifted skirt with abstract floral pattern x got this from one of those thrift stores on crown st back when I was 18 and every girl I knew had a blunt fringe and wore these apparently vintage appearing outfits that oddly looked uncannily homogenous in design right down to the series of variations in pattern n print- I don't know how it's even possible but it is. This skirt belongs to that genus of outfit. Best fit size 6-8.

Price A$20.00

11th August 2020

Item 56:
Swarovski earrings. These are unrelated to Hunter who is actually naturally observant, he has a calm personality. The earrings are a gift from a super observant ex who failed to realize that the reason I never wear earrings is bc I don't act have my ears pierced. They are pretty... gold Swarovski crystals set in a gold-tone drop fixture.

When I was 18, I went and got snake-bite piercings- I know, you would never have guessed it- and I also had my ears pierced at the same time. Eventually, all the piercings closed up after I removed the hardware. I wanted to be distinctive and I guess getting snakebites were a shortcut to being different. But they didn't suit me aha. Some people can pull off piercings. I don't fall within that demographic.

Price A$40.00

11th August 2020

Item 57:
Saks Potts Lucy pink jacket in size 1.

I gave him a coat by this label to give to his mother for her birthday. I loved that coat it was ocean blue and ott fox, I had bought it about two seasons prior but never had a chance to wear it out so it was brand new with tag. I hope she loves the coat n finds an opportunity to wear it, it was spectacular and she is an incredible woman.

I had never met her at that stage but I loved him and wanted him to be happy This jacket I got off matches I think in 2017. Only worn a handful of times and is in pristine condition. If you want to look after the buttons (ie keep them white) either find yourself a decent specialist or use a decent leather cleaner/conditioner or a good moisturizer. Just make sure you don't get it on the shearling n give yourself a disaster. X

Price A$1500.00

11th August 2020

Item 58:
Saks Potts Heart Mongolian fur coat in camel/baby blue: Collection 5, 2016. OS & BNWT. I have access to a specialist furrier in Sydney. Anyone know of one?
I have their Water coat, 2017. Anyone selling the orange colorway??? I think with wear, Mongolian fur fluffs up and loses curl. I read that to restore shape you just wet the fur with water (spray or run thru with your hands-carefully air-dry), as you would with the curls on your head (don't saturate the leather attachment points tho).

Guessing that those who wear their coats thru the snow would probably not encounter this problem? Just don't straight-up dry brush it- unless you want a grand cumulus of frizz. Deadass NOT the thing to do. I was recommended against common sense to dry brush the Water coat back in the day before internet advice in the area was readily found. I thrilled with the result. But I've since happily fixed it by dampening n reshaping the fur. Free postage.

Price A$1000.00 SOLD

19th August 2020

Depop Msg: Eliza x
I know that this is incredibly random, but I just wanted to say that I think the way in which you write is very captivating and beautiful. Im sure you get a few messages commenting on it, I just think that talent like yours

shouldn't go unnoticed! I'm sorry for the pain your ex has put you in and hope that you are now in a better place.

19ᵗʰ August 2020

Reply: Seralita
IBID (mostly)

19ᵗʰ August 2020

Depop Msg: Eliza x
No problem! I can definitely see how it could be therapeutic, I'm a super sentimental person so I love recalling old memories no matter their relation to current situations aha. Hope you had a great day too!

20ᵗʰ August 2020

Item 59:
Escentric molecules Escentric 01: 100ml. Just under half full. A cult favourite BUT reminds me of an ex- not Hunter. Hunter wore Versace Eros. I still remember our first date night- he was dressed in all white and just DOUSED in Versace Eros. At first- being clearly olfactorily uncultured- I thought he had simply gone over vigorous with some variety of Lynx owing to their aggressively successful advertisement campaigns <lynx gets u gurls>. But I grew to love his scent, either becoming acclimatized or he sprayed with more restraint.

Price A$30.00 SOLD

20ᵗʰ August 2020

Item 60:
Jean Paul Gaultier vintage sunglasses, 80s/90s. I had a pair in gold-toned metal that I wore to the beach with Hunter when we went down the South Coast. They got swept into the sea n Hunter gave it his all trying to retrieve it for me, but alas it was lost, and momentarily I thought that perhaps it was foreshadowing of the dynamic of our relationship; I would lose as a result of knowing him.

He was defensive saying that no one wears their glasses into the admittedly somewhat rough surf, but I didn't blame him, it was just the way of it, n it wasn't meant to be I guess, we had an incredible day and I didn't begrudge the loss (although obv did wish I had been less careless) and if it was some universal trade-off- it was worth it to spend that moment in time with him This pair is in pretty much pristine vintage condition.

Price A$500.00

20th August 2020

Depop Comment: Celine Xxxxxx
I'm here for the Hunter stories

20th August 2020

Reply: Seralita
aha thank you for keeping with me lovely xo

20th August 2020

Dennis and I thank you for your support. He used to be jealous of my dog. I can't imagine why. And he once thought of himself as the human-Dennis. I misheard him, The Human Dentist?? I think they already have those- they're called dentists.

Price A$10000000.00

27th August 2020

Depop Msg: Redxxxxx
Hunter the arsehole waved a big red flag admitting he was jealous of the adorable faithful loyal loving Dennis. If I ever cross paths with a dick called Hunter, he'll be kicked back into the kerb in the name of sisterhood. May your heart heal and stay fierce.

27th August 2020

Reply: Seralita
Thank you so much for the solidarity xxx

21st August 2020

Item since removed
He's despicable.

But I love you, I've never desired to be good before I met you and you made me question my resolve and contrarian nature for the better to be brighter lighter and positive like you are and I know that is why wherever you go a thousand hands are helping you at all times. I love you because you are genuine in who you are and never fronted in affection or affectation and I could always see right through to you as you could with me bc I let you in as I had never done before and never will again with another.

Price A$2122018.00

Item 61

27th August 2020

It has touched me to have received so much support and solidarity. Thank you for all your kind msgs xxx I note that some of my descriptions of Hunter May paint him in an unflattering light bc of the unkind and at times galling behaviors that he exhibited towards me in situations that in fairness were difficult to handle but also under situations that were manufactured by a frenemy of mine- and in these circumstances in particular, I feel he could have done better to uphold the proven worth of our relationship over the empty flattery of her poisonous words- but he didn't and cast me aside after all was done and passed- as Jason did Medea (though he wasn't a swindler like Compeyson, I feel much-aligned w Havisham); ultimately Hunter is still the person I fell in love with from day one- and while it may not be apparent- for whom I harbor unreserved care n affection, regardless. If anyone should meet him, please treat him kindly and well; and if you would, *tell him he is a Major ass for the way that he's treated Margaret*

TY- I do mean it x and please be kind to the Hunters in the world, particularly the Hunter aforementioned; tho he may be an ass at times, he is a good ass and an overall kind-hearted man, one who deserves every happiness under the sun x please be gentle w him and w others x

~Unless they offend your sense of justice and self then all bets are off.

Price A$2122018.00

27th August 2020

Depop Msg: NausicaaNoor
Thought all bets were off.. twhaaat dost this remorse speak?

27th August 2020

Reply: Seralita
can't be remorseful when you aint sorry ;) aha I've always significantly held back my more vengeful tendencies when it comes to Hunter x tho probably not in my exposition.. aha it has admittedly been a struggle at times to curb my malice and to maintain care for him through actions the ass but what can you do he remains despite all the person I love.

^I was getting a few msgs about ppl showing support thru violent metaphors and I was worried that I was inspiring potential negativity towards him in a real way- something I definitely don't want to contribute to.

Hence that post x n truthfully, I don't want ppl to hate Hunter or inspire ill-feeling towards him. I just wanted to tell stories and relive memories and share recriminations - a way of venting and also connecting in experience.

27th August 2020

Depop Msg: NausicaaNoor
HahHaaaaaa, yes revenge may feel as though it's ones greatest strength of all, yet sweetness/ love/ compassion triumphs..

Not sure it was clear but yes, you may cause more Karen's than necessary..

Could never cause enough harm to eggs(s) in my opinion.

27th August 2020

Reply: Seralita
Ahahahaha I don't have the heart to act out maximum harshness against Hunter. What are more Karen's? And definitely have plenty more against egg just name the time of day I'm ready to unleash.

28th August 2020

Item 62:
Storytime:
I had an ex let's call him Egg (not Hunter) cast your imagination here on the possible allusions - an aspiring musician let's say who definitely ascribed to notions of

advoc-activism n other female-friendly buzz notes all so that he could slide into a semblance of decency when he was hitting you up for a quick fuck, all while he had a girl/s on the side - meanwhile gaslighting them all- what? No way you're crazy! O That girl?? She Crazy, ignore her- Do you know what it means when a guy claims to have many 'crazy' exes? You don't gotta look far to locate the real crazy.

Nah, the egg doesn't stand for how his car was improved- but if you wanna talk vengeance n malice- let's go there. He sure stood out in traffic as the prettiest ride in Newtown- nothing like love am I rite Egg-o?

The color scheme of this top reminds me of that ^ It's sequined scotch (scotchegg? Hurhur). Best fit size UK6 or 8.

Price A$90.00

28th August 2020

Depop Msg: NausicaaNoor
Toooo good. You're a great writer my friend. I know I've been saying it but I'll say it again. Some female poetry of your experiences please... thinking you should find a publisher actually,, And also, maybe no mention of xxxxxx and filth! I'm convinced these posts will make you famous and maybe (just maybe) (but highly sorta kinda likely maybe) one of those/his girl/s will spot it, just as his xxxxxxxx car stood out in traffic...

28th August 2020

Reply: Seralita
Thank you ! that's so kind of you to say about my writing x n yes I wasn't sure how much I could safely disclose n you're totally right I have now amended the post from hearts n xxxxx to just aha that's vague enough and enough also xx

29th August 2020

Item 63:
A vintage crisp white tiered summer dress with lace and crochet detailing, marked a size M but would best fit size 6-8 (fitted through the top and volume down below). It feels like a cotton lawn material, double lined in cotton I think Thrifted this Not related to Hunter but reminds me of our

uneventual wedding. Unlike Miss Havisham, I refuse to don a wedding gown for the rest of my life, or anything that resembles the form. Like Miss Havisham, I do vow to steep in bitterness and harbor unending resentment until I'm burned alive as the witch that I purportedly am It falls to below my ankles but I am approx 160cm.

Price A$40.00 SOLD

29th August 2020

Item 64:
reserved indefinitely for Jamie who may or may not claim it when the time may or may not come salt never expires It's free to a good home if you can come and pick it up it's not been used only switched on for the photo.

dm me I'm in Sydney n super keen to have this out of my life Otherwise yea free if you cover postage +whatever depop fees- happy to math it out with you Himalayan salt lamp (2-3kg?) marble stand. placed next to my speedy 25 for size reference only.

Given to me by an ex girl friend (non-romantic). It was a toxic relationship. It's gotta go. Authenticated electrical standards-compliant product, wall plug attached It's like brand new as new as salt can be The lamp works fine. It glows from inside the slab of salt. Has purported health benefits, but def not benefiting my health looking at it and thinking about that b*tch. Like a boogey it defies exorcism and refuses to rid itself from my abode where it's distinctly unwelcome- you keen to pick it up?

Price A$20.00 SOLD

29th August 2020

Item 65:
California (Malibu) Pug keyring / bag charm - unused brand new From a friend and ex-housemate that I cannot afford to be sentimental about. Do you love pugs? Do pugs love you? Pugs don't claim to love you - they just do.

Price A$10.00

29th August 2020

Item 66:
Purple jersey mini tank dress with stud beading detail glued on in v good vintage condition. Thrifted in my early 20s.

No relation to Hunter, just don't wear this dress much now- it's very mini in length- like spice girls costume esq - clears my ass by 2 inches- but bc of good manufacturing n material, the dress doesn't ride up/flash ass when I raise my arms.

Would fit size 6-8 (has good stretch- jersey). I think the way I dress has changed throughout the years. Less naked- more layers? I remember telling Hunter that I was probably influenced most heavily in style n aesthetics by relatively modern women- Courtney Love, Alexa Chung n Eva Green- n I recall that he immediately googled for who they are. It kinda surprised me, his earnest interest in knowing who I am, investigating the cultural n ideological spheres that I drew from.

Price A$40.00

29th August 2020

Item 67:
Issey Miyake vintage pleats top. Size M Brand new and unworn Fits me UK6 but yea pleats so I guess up to size UK10 depending on how you wanna style it.

I accordion-bent myself to meet All of his needs. Not anymore. He told me that he never said I love you to any girl that he's been with. He's a 30 yo grown-ass man. What's that a badge of honor?? He told me on multiple occasions that he loved me but then later vehemently denied ever saying it. What the fuck am I right? Why would I make up that shit? I don't think I'm so delusional to have imagined the utterance on more than one, Multiple, occasions Or maybe I am. I loved him/love him. Clearly, I am insane for being so.

Price A$300.00 SOLD

31st August 2020

Item 68:

Safeguard your self;
against fire, thieves, and your bestie

防火防盗防闺蜜

TY ZF

There's no such thing as a sisterhood it's all biological and very logical made up of the full color spectrum of human emotions in its jagged trajectory from the palest to the highest saturation of serration - so guard your heart - or else the cock up will cost.

Price A2122018.00

21st September 2020

Item 69:
Saks Potts Heart jacket (red and white) from collection (I don't remember but it was one before the lake coat) one size brand new with tags x you're welcome.

I hate that he's not here with me and to think of all the retinue of women that he may or may not be with, whom he may or may not be fucking, any of whom he may instead fall in love with and decide to remain with instead of me. I hate when he is delayed in response and cannot help but think it is bc with each passing day that we are apart I matter less and less to him. If I stopped msging if I stopped documenting, would he forget me altogether? If I stopped reminding him would he care to remember who I am? Would he forget me?

Will he come back from across the ocean again for me

Will he come back for me

Will he come back

Will he

21st September 2020

Comment: Seralita

I was recently challenged by a friend who accused me of doing everything that I did for Hunter bc I wanted to secure his love, that my support of him was in some way flawed and false bc he suggested, therefore, it was conditional and therefore it was fundamentally a form of manipulation, as I fundamentally wanted something from Hunter.

I disagree. Of course I desire H's love. The desire to receive affection and consideration is only natural of our or any relationship. But it doesn't therefore reduce my actions thru my support of him, as somehow impure and conditional. The two conditions exist simultaneously. I know without a doubt that I love him and want the best for him n do what I know how to support him, though perhaps too often from my stubborn viewpoint. I know for certain that I would never knowingly try to buy/or in some way manipulate his love- and wouldn't desire this if it wasn't sincere but was instead something wrought through magic and artifice.

Sure I don't do it all out of benevolence- I'm not made of infinite time, resourcefulness and resources. I do it For Him bc I love him. Would be ace if his despicable ass loves me back. Would make me sad if he doesn't.

But I made the choice and I rolled the dice on him out of love. I would still make the same choices if I had the chance to do-over.

#love

26th September 2020

Depop Msg: lolaxxxxxx
I'm living for these lil stories

Stop selling all your cool clothes, I bet Hunter isn't half as cool as you or the clothes or the prose.

26th September 2020

Reply: Seralita
Aha thanks for the encouragement x Hunter's an incredible man that's why he's so dear to me, but you're right I'm wayyy cooler.

Seralita's Depop: Havisham.Medea

27th September 2020

Shop   Likes   Saved   Reviews

A catalogue of heartbreak

> **Active today**   > **76 Sold**

Bio: Constant gripe with my friend Hunter, I think he's acted despicably, I also love him very much

https://instagram.com/medea.havisham

238 followers
7 following

Part two: Bile

Interlude I

17th July 2020

Text Msgs
From: Margaret
To: Hunter

And I curse you from now to forever. In days near or far you will experience the same suffering as unexpectedly and for as long as I will and live to dread it, count on it, in any and all that you meet. By air and darkness, across land and sea, black dragons to drown the sun for me, and no light will penetrate with the passing of each day after day after terrible day. Be cast and be blighted by the ardors of love.

I curse you to match my tears for equal sorrow to never find rest until my plight is lifted from now to the end of time in this life and the next and the next until the rain flows back skywards and the seasons turn on their heads when mountains uproot into moors and the sun takes its last breath. Near and far. And barrenness to all who touch you. Go forth.

You will never feel warmth and know its certitude. Tenderness will always remain out of your reach. By air and darkness my will be done. Black dragons drown the sun. A hole that runs through and through from now to ever until my heart should move. Near and far, land and sea, air and darkness, from all four quarters they will seek. Until the Phoenix joins the Dragon in the sky, so let my words' effect take flight. Sic fiat semper.

Black waters and ruin to all that you touch. Go forth and go forth and go forth. I curse you to wander but never find, to see all but never avoid, to break all that you touch and to know and know and know all of the calamitous ruin you wreak. Until the two meet in the sky, to last until the end of time.

May all your crops fail. Sour milk and stillbirth to haunt you like an inseverable placenta. All fine things to your firstborn but the ability to feel sated. To your second-born, to feel but not hold the weight of tragedies. To all she who stand by you, consumption to all her losses, and of which the retinue will never stand still until the carousel runs empty of visitors. From when you should touch upon the bite of steel may this charm be placed. No words or counter may undo its bonds to last until the end of time. Only when my heart is moved, or when the phoenix joins the dragon in the sky where the rain flows skywards, and the seasons turn on their heads when mountains uproot into moors and the sun takes its last breath.

Whoever should stay by you will wear the ruin of it like a thick suit of stagnancy, unshifting and unyielding until they are parted from you. Find your joy in yourself alone.

Interlude II

20th July 2020

Email
From: Margaret
To: Hunter
You Go do whatever you want but first give me back my ring. I will pursue actions against you otherwise. I don't want anything to do with you or anything sullied by your memory.

21st July 2020

Email
From: Margaret
To: Hunter
You asked for me to hate you as I am known to hate others. But I didn't have it in me before. You're despicable, dishonest to cut and go each time shutting me out after all is done. If you won't make amends, then be cursed for it I don't have it in me to be magnanimous or to forgive.

25th July 2020

Email
From: Margaret
To: Hunter
Tell that Korean bitch to stop hitting me up I've made my settings so that all calls to private numbers go directly to voicemail.

Screenshot
From: Margaret
To: Hunter

\<No Caller ID\> Unknown	**12:17am** (i)
\<No Caller ID\> Unknown	**12:16am** (i)
\<No Caller ID\> Unknown	**Yesterday** (i)
\<No Caller ID\> Unknown	**Yesterday** (i)
\<No Caller ID\> Unknown	**Yesterday** (i)
\<No Caller ID\> Unknown	**Yesterday** (i)

<No Caller ID> Unknown	Yesterday	(i)
<No Caller ID> Unknown	Yesterday	(i)
<No Caller ID> Unknown	Yesterday	(i)

Voicemail: 26

25th July 2020

Email
From: Hunter
To: Margaret
I managed to harass my mother back in the United States enough to mail your precious ring back, it should arrive by August 4th. Both of you can now leave me the fuck alone. Maybe instead of worrying about the ring, you can worry about getting psychiatic counseling, or family counseling. Don't email again.

25th July 2020

Email
From: Hunter
To: Margaret
NOW LEAVE ME THE FUCK ALONE WITH YOUR PSYCHO SHIT

25th July 2020

Email
From: Margaret
To: Hunter
You're an ungrateful abusive emotionally bankrupt disloyal parasitic person who has no place to comment on my emotional wellbeing which was drastically compromised by your actions, and in turn, severely damaged my family, you have no place to comment on what we should or should not do. You should focus on your own bullshit with your Korean Japanese or whoever bitches instead of worrying about that. I hope my curse against you finds its bite. Go fuck yourself.

29th July 2020

Email
From: Margaret
To: Hunter

You knew who and what I am from the start as I made no disguise about this.

The ugliness of this detailed charm is an expression of the white anger that I experienced over your actions, which I found deplorable.

Yet this charm could never have worked and was always void, as you are and have always been protected by an earlier charm that I had unwittingly placed upon the both of us when I barely even knew you. If you believe in charms and curses, you would know that they are only merely vessels for the transference of energy. They are directed by intent, contained within linguistic parameters, and fettered only by the limitations of one's imagination and mastery of metaphor. It was Wittgenstein who said the limits of my language mean the limits of my world.

I meant for my language to be laced with barbs. I wanted to impress upon you the depths of the hurt that you have inflicted on me.

I loosen my curse against you. Curses cast cannot be undone but I call on night and rain to loosen the charm that holds fast so that it may dilute with each drop of rain and grow less jagged by the borrowed shade of this night. By air and darkness, I call on the four watchtowers with my familiar to bear witness and hold vessel while the rain pours and unscorches the air to loosen the bonds that hold together this charm. May what love that remains in my heart shelter you from the reaches of this curse to dissolve into sea foam with the dawn. Nox lux pox pax ergo in infinitum. Odi et amo.

Interlude III

8th September 2020

Unspoken of, or perhaps less popular in the broader forum of contemporary discourse are those narratives that seem to cast doubt on the pink lining of the sisterhood and its sorority of women-in-arms, there to catch each other, support each other, bolster each other- a united front against the supposed villainy of the guy – ready with fierce battle cries:

- You Go Gurl! YAS Queen! BYE BOY!-

Sorry. It is always more nuanced.

The first thing that bitch did after a moment of conflict between she and me- after she reassured me that she had blocked and deleted him on my express request - supposedly she claimed out of loyalty and respect for me when I had told her that I couldn't tolerate any trace of association with him in my life- she IMMEDIATELY reached out to him to share the piteous story of what a victim she was (what was said in detail I could only imagine as I was not privy to their dms)

- oh, poor her-

And I know how she would have framed it. She had done this on a previous occasion: she had taken it upon herself to specifically reach out to him to let him know that I had stopped being friends with her- supposedly over a fight concerning him- and that although she was saddened by this, still wished me well and hoped that he would take care to not hurt me.

She knew full well the consequences of how her message would be interpreted by him, while he and I were having issues at the time. About the conflict between her and me, he had no frame of reference or context, as I had always kept him separate from it, never brought it up. She knew that he would interpret my actions as seemingly unreasonable or even unstable. By portraying herself as the victim and extending a seemingly magnanimous request for him to avoid hurting me, she had with a single brushstroke painted herself as the victim and tarred me as the aggressor.

The purpose of her message was to prompt an automatic response in him, to cause him to distance himself from me. She knew that he would react in this way, banking on his assumption that I was acting out and making wild decisions due to the supposed clouding of my judgement triggered by my heightened feelings towards him. She knew that he was kind and that he would respond this way out of his care for my wellbeing. She had designed the situation to that effect.

This time, her actions prompted him to re-add her and then delete me from his social media- which to be honest, I don't give a fuck about as I had only reactivated my accounts to have a backup means of staying in contact with him when he was fucked up injured overseas and had lost his bank cards and phone. Through her actions, what was made clear is that: a) she was always using her influence over him as a means to manipulate a response in me and b) he was gullible enough to side with her and her manipulative bullshit over me.

She needs to stay the FUCK out of my life. Any friend, whether they are your girlfriend, bestie, or close friend, should know better than to interfere in the finer moments and the private dynamics of your actual partner-relationship. Not to proffer supposed advice or unsolicited 'aid' to you or (WORSE) to your partner. As a wise person, one should know better than to trust in 'friends' who do this.

While she and I were still friends, this bitch dressed up her intentions and actions as 'trying to help,' all the while gaslighting me the entire time when I had felt (rightly) that her influence had overstepped natural boundaries. It upsets me that on multiple occasions he has failed to: a) notice b) object and also c) when he sided with her and was sympathetic to her plight while dismissive of my mine when I attempted to explain the circumstances to him as I caught on to what was happening, as I realized the truth of my relationship with her. But I can't blame him too harshly, as I had been fooled repeatedly by her also.

Under no conditions will I tolerate her in my life.

Her actions were the very definition of gaslighting. She would incept and normalize dynamics and ideas, slowly, imperceivably, over time like boiling a frog, to inculcate within me an intimacy that was neither natural nor true. And when I came to doubt the veracity, she would deny deny deny.

She first came into my life during a moment of vulnerability and would make inroads from that point onwards, always during moments of weakness in my guard, against the times of emotional upheaval in my life, during which she would position herself as a best friend, a sister.

This time around, I had cut her off for effectively 9-months before she came back into the fold, riding the waves of grief from my heart following the death of my gran. Hunter had passed on to her the knowledge that my gran had passed away on February 12th, 2020- believing that this girl truly cared for me and in the possibility of repairing a friendship between she and me- as he never truly understood the context between us. And against this backdrop of disorienting grief, coupled with the simultaneously unfolding global COVID-19 pandemic, she made contact with me and I let down my guard once more- to my folly- and let her back into my life.

In retrospect, I can see all the moments of her gaslighting, how she would justify it and turn the issue around into something else. I remember when she had asked him to model for her, to be the anatomical model for her to locate acupuncture points on his body. And how she blatantly overstepped the boundaries unnecessarily tracing and lingering her hands against his body right in front of my face and flirting openly with him, and him responding positively to her thickly lavished flattery. I remember that I was furious- not only because I had agreed to the session among the three of us on her request to assist her in her revision of point location to pass an upcoming assessment- but because I couldn't verbalize the deep affront that I felt towards what was happening in front of my goddamn face. And I remember I stormed out of the restaurant later that night, leaving the two of them behind.

On a separate occasion, she later 'counselled' me, that he was in fact confused and couldn't understand the way I had behaved and the intensity of my emotions that night. And that in fact it was I who had transgressed for not 'giving him face' in public in front of my friends, and for instead 'chucking a tantrum.' What a slap in the face! She had managed to both conveniently re-package what had happened and turn the fault back around on me, as well as completely undermine my perception and grasp of reality.

She had overstepped the FUCK out of the boundaries- while both of them proceeded to claim innocence in even awareness of the deliberate and flagrant transgression.

    -What was the purpose behind her actions?-

You may ask me. Why would she do all this when in fact she didn't truly care for or even love him, and nor was she trying to claim him for her own.

Her purpose was to test my limits and to maintain control over me through him, to maintain the status quo of her friendship with me. She purposefully interplaced herself within the relationship between him and me because she recognized that it had the potential to surpass the depth and challenge the veracity of the friendship between her and me.

Maybe she sees it all going down differently. Who knows? After all, the truth is multi-faceted and pluralistic in this post-modern world.

So, go ahead, hit her up and ask her. Maybe she's got a ripe story ready to justify all of her actions. Ask her to write it all down even. Her retelling of it. I don't care to know either it or her.

Part three: Beginnings

21st December 2018

Le chasseur de fleurs

You will fly soon, and I will dive,
Into deepest blue to find the
Red amongst white stars
O Wanderer you travel far to
Store the stories, gazes, memories
To fill golden blooms before fade;

Cross the Pacific back in time
Tell me a story, become mine,
Over mountains, over lakes,
Glory to light and create,
Resist the Shadow that falls in between
Do not go gentle, recall your dreams,
Reach and risk and rise to make,
Let me build and let me break,
How many hundred visions and revisions,
Questions and choices and indecisions,
A fabric of motion and stars a crown,
The moon concedes the dawn and she
Lies down.

Lita to Hunter, 2018

A matter of yuanfen

Hunter and I met for the first time on 2nd December 2018. I remember the day distinctly.

I had got off a train at Central Station. I had travelled from the International Terminal of Sydney airport, where I was joined by my office in performing a send-off for a dear colleague and friend who had, in the two years of knowing him, gone above and beyond to help me achieve significant milestones in both my career and academic study. We were never involved but there was always a question and a possibility which went unexplored for reasons that would not be overcome.

Saying goodbye to him, I was overwhelmed with sadness. He was returning to his home country. It was the point of divergence in our lives. I knew, although he promised in earnest that he would keep in touch, that the friendship would never be as close from that moment onwards. I was aware that we were parting forever. It would be a long time (if ever?) before we would meet again. And by then we would be very different people, possibly strangers to one another.

A friend came to meet me at Central Station when I got off the train. I cried in his car while he comforted me. He listened to me for a long time and afterwards gave me a lift to the neighbouring suburb.

I walked along Crown St in Surry Hills and reflected on the time in the past when I took my colleague there. I had always intended to bring him to Low302, which I had frequented in my early 20s as a familiar haunt and the site of many affectionate memories. Unfortunately, at that time Low was under refurbishment. The doors were closed so instead we went elsewhere.

That night though, by providence perhaps, Low302 was open for business and I decided to go inside, compelled by a sense of nostalgia, and a longing to feel safe within the walls that once contained so many fond experiences.

Lost in thought, I stumbled on the threshold; I had accidentally caught the stiletto of my heel in the crack on the floor. And lovely Mel appeared out of nowhere to apologize and check if I was alright.

   -Yes I am, thank you, just being a ditz tonight –

I made my way inside to the bar and that was when I met him as he stood behind the counter, looking ripped in a T, dressed in top to bottom black, probably in his 20s, smiled, looked me directly in the eye, and asked me what I was having that night.

   -I don't know, I just said goodbye to someone forever-

Like a bird in a storm, somehow, without realizing it, I was carried on strange currents into his life. He spent the night talking to me while my thoughts wandered from Low to where I knew the flight was about to take off. I time-travelled back and forth and maintained polite interest as he spoke to me and was kind to me, and I drifted in and out of awareness of this. I had a vague sense that he was engaging with me in earnest, but I was also doubtful – as I always am with my hardened view of all men- of his character as he is young (I'm 29- he volunteered when I had not asked) and a bartender on a working visa.

He told me he was creating a new drinks menu and was kind to me and spent the majority of the time explaining the details as he formulated cocktails that he imagined I might enjoy. One of the drinks was named in his honor; Le chasseur de fleurs.

He took off the charge when it came to the tab, and when I left him a tip I could see the conflict written on his face and I sensed something honest in him, and in the slight note of anxiety when he double confirmed, as I was leaving, that the number I had written for him on a paper napkin was indeed correct and mine.

I asked him where he was from.

         -I'm from Boston, Massachusetts, USA-

         -All the good ones are always taken-

He said, partially in jest when I explained the circumstances that had preceded and ultimately brought me there that night.

***

The next night when I met him on a date- that I didn't know was a date until much later on when he confirmed to the waiter at the Winery who was also his friend.

-yea it's my night off and it's date night-

And okay sure I got it at that point.

I remember how I initially thought that perhaps he was gay; he was dressed in all white and slightly fidgeting and just DOUSED in aftershave. He told me that he had rode his bike over.

- oh cool-

I wasn't sure whether he was trying to impress me- or even of the type of bike he meant push or motor.

He told me that as he worked in hospitality, he would cut slack for the many friends he made in the field, and vice versa they would do the same for him- like a band of brothers. We went from the Winery back to Low for a drink on his off-night and he was a bit awkward because Aref was there and I think also Daniel Johns who is a regular. It was indeed a bit awkward, and so we left.

I think he got a pizza? and then either a wine or a beer from the bottle-o - I can't remember which now- to bring back to his. I remember that I wasn't hungry that night. I remember that I didn't want to drink and declined his several offers to buy me one and this appeared to throw him off. I had wanted to stay sober because I didn't want to come off as just another girl fishing for free drinks or to be drinking on the regular- particularly when I didn't need to be drunk to make my decision to go back with him that night.

I remember testing him, asking:

-So what's your five-year plan?-

Which in my mind is the most mundane question you could bring on a date, but also the most intriguing. The response has the potential to reveal facets of the respondent's character. Would they answer in earnestness? Would they mock the basicness of the question and deride you for asking it? Would they indeed rattle off prestigious career milestones? Would they respond defensively for being asked the question and reflect this through animosity and barbed retorts? Are they reading into the question and prepared to immediately judge you? Would they lie through their teeth to try to impress you? Are they trying to seduce you, woo you, entice you, build an empire of lies around you- just so that they can fuck you?

We were sat on a bench and I was trying to decide whether he was genuine- or even interested- because he seemed oddly not forward as I had perhaps expected of this tall ripped looking man who must (I assumed) have good success pulling girls and women as he is a bartender with a cute smile.

I told him that there was a concept in Chinese:

-Yuanfen-

It is an idea of fated destiny: a match in the present born out of a connection in the past. A unique pairing out of the countless possibilities. In a moment of cynicism, I told him that all of life was a performance:

-We are all actors on a stage, preparing a face to meet the faces that you meet-

And he told me in earnestness that he didn't like that thought. And that was the moment I accepted that he was an honest person and decided that I would let down my walls and stop playing my mind games and reciprocate in truth the openness that he had shown me without reservation.

He asked me to describe myself in a few words or using a proverb and I told him:

-Still water runs deep-

He fucked me twice. In the morning after, I kissed him on the forehead and walked out of his place without looking back.

-Good luck with everything-

I told him as I departed and later sent him a clip of Glow by Digitalism while I caught the train home.

I was joined at one of the stops by Kang, a different colleague who always held my respect in confidence. We travelled together and reflected on the events over the past two days; the departure of our colleague and the unexpected circumstances that had led me to meet Hunter.

4th December 2018

Conversation
Between Kang and Margaret

Margaret: I dunno, he seems nice, I guess? Maybe a bit lonely?
Kang: It is special that you and he met that night. Maybe he is special.
Margaret: Yea, I don't think so. I dunno if I'll see him again.

All that he has given to me, I would never sell or throw away. I close down my rooms and every clock at the minute of the hour to never pass until either white covers me or black takes me while the feast wilts on bronzed silver dusted with rust. And yet hopefully, I yearn for it to come sooner and wistfully look to the East which means so many things and is not so far away. I'm just waiting, although I may have changed my attire, it is only until I perish in fire, or as promised, let the ocean claim me.

***

The present his Kris Kringle had got him was a hugely oversized yellow novelty mug emblazoned with bolded black text SIZE MATTERS. It came with a necklace made up of ridiculously oversized wooden beads - clearly an in-joke- a reference to his impressively ripped physique. The present he had prepared for his own Kris Kringle, which I had helped him wrap, was Po-Chai and Po-Sum - courtesy of yours truly once again. I gave him a ride to Terminus where I dropped him off to join his workmates at the end-of-year Christmas party that was being thrown by his old boss.

I watched him get ready. He was dressed in all white for the occasion, despite my well-meaning caveat that he was bound to spill wine onto his outfit at some stage during the night, as it was a wide opportunity for Murphy's Law to be demonstrated.

He wore a cut-off tank with 'Happy Lift-Mas' written in red print (another in-joke referencing his physique, built through committed dedication to a gym routine), white pants, Converse lace-ups, and the outfit was topped off with a Santa hat. I expected that he would enjoy the night with his friends, to continue into the afterparty. Meanwhile, I would spend my night at home with my parents, with whom I was living at the time. I was looking forward to the opportunity unwind after having spent several days together, living with him.

He messaged me later unexpectedly that night, to come back for him, to pick him up, and so I made the 45-min drive back into the CBD at approaching 10pm, to pick his drunk ass up while dodging the intently disapproving glare of my parents as I left again- they had perhaps expected my recently returned company to stay a little longer.

It was later, after I had picked him up, while I was driving back to his, that he told me; at some point during the night he had made out with Lucy, his co-worker. He just blurted it out of the blue, voluntarily but defensively, clearly expecting a backlash. I didn't know what to say. I hadn't expected the information that he had just dropped on me.

-We're just friends yea? -

He was always quick to deflect the intimacy of our relationship. Truthfully, I was a little bit bothered, and immediately cast in my mind the scene of him in the arms of a faceless yet also gorgeous woman, and felt somewhat put-off and wondered- perhaps as a natural response in these types of situations- is she hotter than me? I was confused by why he had chosen to tell me this and to just blurt it out when he knew that the information had the potential to provoke an inflammatory response in me, and surely in any partner. And yet something in his response felt organic and disarmingly unfiltered. I didn't hold his actions against him, and later he proceeded to fuck me into the night.

I met Lucy later at a different party with Hunter, back at Low302, when he returned to Australia for me. She and I flirted a bit- I think she is bi? But I'm not. It was the first and only time I met her; Hunter had invited his friends to join him at Low for a farewell. It was his last night in Sydney- again.

I didn't hold any reservations against her. I was genuinely interested in finally meeting her and I think she and I got on well. That night it was apparent that Hunter was with me. I remember that I made a conscious effort to ensure that she was included in conversations among our friends, as I felt that she was probably only familiar with Hunter, and perhaps didn't get on particularly smoothly with the others. Especially with Nathan, who at some point during the night engaged her in a semi-heated discussion over the topic of whether dick size mattered (FYI guys, it do- aha). At some point, an international chart of dicks was googled and passionately debated over.

***

I still remember the first time he left Australia and left me.

He passed on all his possessions that he could not bring with him, onto me; the lamp, drape, bedding, mug, jacket, Vienna press, print, a set of coasters marked with symbolism of marital compatibility. At some point early on I felt myself let down my guard and let go of my cynicism and open my heart to him, in a way that I had never done before, with unmitigated sincerity. And I made the decision that I would do everything I could to keep him safe from harm.

I don't know why I felt this way. But I don't regret this.

Perhaps that is #love

The complications that arose between Hunter and I are unique, but also, perhaps, mundane. We are separated by an ocean; he is in USA, while I am in Sydney, Australia.

At some point during our relationship, he decided to move on, to stop entertaining the possibility of coming back for me, that it was necessary to stop maintaining the same level of intimacy in our relationship because he had decided that it was too much for him to handle. I think perhaps this is why he consistently broke up with me, time and time again. Yet afterwards, we would try and try over. I do not know. I would reach out to him, and on occasions, he would reach out to me, and we would try once again. But it was always unclear, I suppose to the both of us, as we never spoke of the boundaries of our relationship and what we desired from each other.

The reason I keep reaching out to him is that I never stopped loving him. I do not know why he reaches out to me. I do not know if he will continue to remain in contact with me.

I wish I could be more strategic, to 'tone it down' as he has so often pleaded with me, to be less intense. I feel like my actions have always been transparent in the undeniable sentiment that they embody.

Is this an obsession to feel so strongly for him; have I just simply imagined the depth of connection when it is not there or possibly never was?

I've always felt a sense of conflict within him, and not necessarily limited to the scope and expression of our relationship, but rather a personal conflict; something within himself that remains unresolved, which imparts on him, to the casual observer at least, the impression of appearing seemingly irresolute.

Going through my message logs, I found a conversation between myself and his housemate, from earlier on in our relationship. The conversation captures my reflection on what I had interpreted as a sense of ambivalence within him. Perhaps this ambivalence is what attracted me to him initially and brought me close to him in my curiosity to find out who he is, and eventually led me to open my heart completely to him.

FB Msger

Margaret: Hey Oscar, how are you? I have a question, relating to Hunter, could I please ask you?
May 2, 2019, 4:32 AM

Oscar: Hi Margaret, I am very well thank you. How about you? sure, you can ask me.
May 2, 2019, 4:45 PM

Margaret: Thanks for getting back to me :) The question I wanted to ask, is probably a bit unanswerable. I guess I was in a bit of a bind because I wasn't sure whether he ever cared for/loved me. I think I got the answer from speaking to Hunter. So embarrassing/awkward. But yeah. thanks for getting back to me
May 2, 2019, 4:47 PM

Oscar: No worries, hope you are ok with the answer you got. :)
May 2, 2019, 4:49 PM

Margaret: Tbh we keep going around in circles. Like figure 8. but maybe that says something too.
May 2, 2019, 4:50 PM

Oscar: It is difficult for me to say because I did not really know much about your relationship but I think that the best way to find out, is to talk honestly and accept whatever outcome.
May 2, 2019, 4:53 PM

Margaret: I think I perceive dissonance among the words he says to me and his actions/behaviors. He keeps trying to tell me that he doesn't love me/but it goes against how I feel he acts. So I don't know. But yeah clearly I'm fond of him, so yeah we keep going around. Anyway. Thank you for your advice. I really appreciate it and hope everything is well with you.
May 2, 2019, 4:57 PM

Oscar: No worries, hope things get better. likewise. :)
May 2, 2019, 4:59 PM

I was told that I do indeed want love and seek connection, no matter what I say. I was recommended to the plenty of other amazing people. It was suggested that I may be surprised by how quickly one can change their mind and perspective on what they want... that it is okay to dip into different waters, that's what life is for Discovery, Exploration, Enjoyment.

<Paraphrased: Text msg from NausicaaNoor, 30th September 2020>

I don't dispute this. But I also maintain that there is something valuable in remaining fixed, remaining devoted, so to speak. And this unique value is frequently overlooked, while the virtues of moving on are generally extolled as the 'healthy' way to go forward, to lead one's 'best life.'

I might take this opportunity now to clarify that this is the reason I identify with the Dickensian Miss Havisham character. The resonance I find isn't with the bitterness that corrupts her and eventually poisons those closest to her- that is her tragedy. In what is probably a drastic departure from the text, I read deeply into her capacity for relentless bitterness and identify within it an implicit character trait; the rare potential to give completely out of devotion to love and in defiance of all persuasion.

This concept was obviously not explored in the narrative. Miss Havisham's potential for love was unfortunately distorted by her inability to handle the injustice of the circumstances that she had been cast into. Yet, in another context, that strength of relentless devotion, as seen in her choice to remain fixed in time rather than to take the easier, less cost-invested decision to let go and move on, would demonstrate unique heroism. Whether the cost of that decision is worthwhile would be contingent upon the trueness of the love that the sacrifice was being made for. Yet that doesn't mitigate the implicit heroism in the ability to remain ardent when one is seemingly cast into darkness.

Apparently, the actual historical person that Miss Havisham was based upon retreated from the world and lived in deliberate disarray, yet still kept her front door permanently ajar, in hopes of receiving her departed love should he one day return to her.

The situation is unmistakeably sad and speaks of a lifetime of opportunities lost and a life retreated from. Yet it also suggests a very enduring hope, one which bore a very real and raw potential to withstand the weathering of doubt and difficulty- all for the sake of realizing the possibility of a very specific love and connection.

***

To clarify my intentions behind producing this text, I note that it is inescapable for this endeavour to be divorced from the influence by my underlying hope to be closer to Hunter. This remains the heart of my desire.

Yet I feel the need to emphasize that this body of work was never designed to coerce him, to be wielded as an instrument of persuasion, or vengeance.

In some way, this shop on Depop has been a vehicle for me to document and make sense of my experiences, to understand myself, and the depth and enduring tensility of my attachment to Hunter. This was explored through interactions with many others; friends, strangers, through the threads of different conversations facilitated by the transnational platform of this shopping app. In the pursuit of fashion (buying, selling, appraising, and donning), I assuage my heartache and temporarily displace my desire.

I would not be open to another relationship if it is not with him. I am past caring to seek validation and am too tired to start and maintain the potential connections that could be gained through knowing another. I was involved, briefly, barely and intermittently, and while I was with this man- who is distinctly different from Hunter- I noted that he would often (well-meaningly and without arrogance) reassure me of my attractiveness, and his attraction to me, through various adjectives and endearments. It confused me- because who asked?

I don't want to be going through the dance with someone or many people, to be picking through, liking, developing whatever connections and transmissions because of the biology of attachment and the experience of the intellectual bond until either a truer connection is formed or perhaps when sufficient flattery has been lavished.

There is something between me and Hunter. It is hard for us because of time, distance, and geography. Yet nothing is without potential. I insist on being true to seeing it through rather than putting it down and moving on simply because that is what I'm told is the trend as a healthy course of action. Who could tell? I don't think anyone or any institution holds the key or answer to those particular questions- rather we create the paths to our lives by our unique decisions. I choose to remain loyal to the sincerity of my sentiments.

Perhaps having a partner would bring certain pragmatic benefits. But I want something specific, and I already know what that is.

I don't know if there's necessarily a right or wrong way about it. Perhaps my choices delay me in my progression through life and subvert my ability to experience true happiness. Perhaps I too will be corrupted as Miss Havisham was, because that is the only natural course of outcome in the case of a broken heart in one who remains steadfast to their sense of devotion. Perhaps because of this I won't meet natural benchmarks and milestones. And yet I want something specific, that only I can be certain of.

***

-I don't want my racehorse fat-

He told me about this past-the-prime white dude he met in South East Asia who spoke of women as though they're thoroughbreds.

-they gotta have developed muscle, toned but not too ripped, good hips, perky breasts, thick hair mmm fertile- but not too fat-

He asked me if I would still stand by him if he got sloppy and crusty and old and decrepit.

-of course-

I wasn't with him because of his religious gym attendance, but I said I would always want him to be happy and I knew that if he were in poor condition that would affect his outlook and so I would actively support efforts to improve his wellbeing- which I guess is a vaguely political answer- and perhaps not the response that he was looking for, which was a more disciplinarian approach to snap him back into shape if he ever became complacent- as all couples become when they enter into relationships in his opinion (and he cares very much about presenting a great rig).

I think I would be more subtle in my approach, but to be honest I agree with him.

> - Na I put in too much work to be with someone who doesn't make an effort-

He replied in earnest when I asked whether he would be with girls who didn't look after themselves and I get it 100%. Warhorses can't be fat. I wouldn't expect less of him than to reach the bar that I've set for myself. But that's probably not true; I've made many exceptions for him.

He has a softer heart than I have. He would never be able to sever ties as decisively and comprehensively as I am known to do- always for strong reasons of course- because he is kinder, more generous, unwilling to explore the harsher motivations of the unscrupulous and the callous. Sometimes I feel protective of him for this because I, on the other hand am too aware of the trips and traps and shortcomings- and I'm often compelled to take to battle for him, to front and bear teeth- always with a smile (because I'm still a girl and aren't they delicate and sweet) to keep him from harm, shielded from the jaws of the world.

I don't think I am a hard person. But in the face of injustice, I can be relentless in the pursuit of its restoration. I blasted him without holding back my exposition with the full weight of my force and uncurbed language which he couldn't handle- and how could he possibly? What hope does a carefree breeze carry to change the course of a hurricane of fury? But storms pass. And we remain. Always.

A correspondence

21st August 2020

Depop Msg: Scintalla
The 9 of swords noooo but the fool is for new beginnings so hope maybe? Hope you're doing well.

Reply: Seralita
Hey, lovely xx thanks for reaching out. I'm doing alright x hope you are also. I actually msged Hunter a few days ago, as a research paper to which I invited his assistance on has been accepted for publication :) He and I are both listed co-authors aha super proud of him it's his first (I know- aha the love don't fade).
I hope you are doing well also. Whatever it is, you can get through you might not be happier, but who knows, maybe it'll come around again and better. x

Depop Msg: Scintalla
That's crazy omg I hope everything goes well with the research paper! May I ask what it's about (if that's not too nosy lol! I love research and theses) and I'm doing well, thank you for the love sending some right back.

Reply: Seralita
Thank you! You are too sweet the paper is an animal study on the therapeutic applications of a particular herbal medicine, in neuropharmacology aha snore snore x Take care! Am blessed to know you thru this xo

23rd August 2020

Depop Msg: Scintalla
That's fascinating! I'm a psych major so I love reading studies and gleaning information (inductive reasoning) curious as to why it's an animal study. Is it unethical to get humans involved or animals the first stage? And yes, wow I'm also blessed to know you and get to talk to you! Honored you feel that way.

Reply: Seralita
That's amazing! I love reading on psychology :) I studied fine art/philosophy n have a masters in traditional Chinese medicine, currently a PhD candidate in the latter x

Hunter is a biological engineering graduate, way more scientific than I am aha. Yea with evidence-based scientific research, before anything gets to clinical practice, it needs to go thru a lot of appraisals- lab and animal studies are at the lower end of the level of evidence pyramid (randomized controlled trials n meta-analysis at the top- to inform clinical practice guidelines.) xo It's rough to do animal studies in many cases :(but there are ethical parameters in place to reduce suffering where possible.

Depop Msg: Scintalla
That's !! amazing that you got to study fine art, philosophy and traditional Chinese medicine and you get to apply it too....and lmao @ Hunter being a STEM major. I wonder if he's one of those atheist white boys with egalitarian/libertarian bc I've met a few And yes, there's so much red tape in research! It's necessary but I'm not very interested in the research side of things.... I have no idea what I'm going to do about my future. It's not bleak, just foggy.

Reply: Seralita
Aha there's a Lot of red tape in research! I was never really scientifically minded/research-driven, but rather as I studied more n worked, it seemed that more doors/developments opened up in that direction- I was never that methodical/w a clear focus in life aha (some people are n are perhaps more ahead??) But learning it, it's def a useful n versatile skill whether ultimately, I end up in the field or not it's def a pathway to career development (in Aus at least n also perhaps in USA?)

Aha Hunter is a STEM major but he's not one of those liberal/art-house/musician white boys (I've dated several). The type that likes to front by name-checking great thinkers/movements/music/whatever other forms of social currency only as a shallow veneer to appear more refined/intelligent/elegant- in order to feel a bit more secure when they're in the midst of a crowd or when they're pulling girls. It's funny that you should mention this!

Hunter is unique and escaped my initial profile (super buff bartender - I thought he would be cocky n soo smooth in his game); he's actually disarmingly gentle and unpresuming, without pretension. I saw it immediately n opened myself to him because I could see that his heart is kind. Xxx

Hit me up if you're ever in Sydney, Aus (when the COVID lifts) my number (+61 xxx xxx xxx) xo

28th August 2020

Depop Msg: Scintalla
The scientific aspect of research is a drag!! I'm more of the philosophical, argumentative type haha I'm good w thinking (and I apologize for not replying earlier, the semester began on Monday and it's been a Lot! I also hope I'm not taking up too much of your time with your messages, lol!) And I'm glad Hunter is not that way! There are way too many of those men out there and I would like some variety, please.

He kinda reminds me of the last guy I was semi-involved with (situationships! lol!) and it took me foreverrrr to get over this self-absorbed lonely fool of a being. A part of me still wants revenge for how I was treated and how much I suffered in the relationship but he's the type that doesn't really learn his lessons, so I'll leave it up to karma, I guess?

And I'm not sure if you're serious about hitting you up if/when I'm in Sydney but one of my boyfriend's friends lives there so it might be a very real possibility if/when we visit.

Reply: Seralita
Definitely, research can be snore-city, dry bc you're literally sifting thru a heap of technical language n data but yea there's a pay off at some point... far off in the distance aha a vague/great sense of achievement aha. It sounds like you're passionate about what you're doing tho which is so awesome! Yea w vengeance I think it's kinda to each their own. I've always looked to the classics for how to ease heartache and mete out justice- or Vengeance! aha.

It sucks tho that you were w someone who caused you suffering :(I do believe in doing what it takes to right where I have been wronged aha until you feel alright again - which sounds a bit scary but I act don't have the heart to cause true suffering. I like to deal out a dash of poetic justice just here and there.

In the case of an ex (not Hunter), I improved his car w pastel graff w a gf one night- he never figured it out tho as he had too many girls he had pissed off at the time that he could only speculate as it could have been any or several of the women he was seeing at the time. It's probably not the most legally sound thing to do aha but it sure was satisfying.

No regrets at all aha Whatever it is tho, prob try not to waste your time and life on those who aren't worth it, in order to prove it to them/show it to them. Cos it's your life (lived in however which way you choose happily or unhappily) and ultimately it'll be an experience that you will look back on as something singular and valuable x N for sure :) I do mean it, hit me up if you're in Syd x would be so special to meet in the future!

The week has been good I act spoke with Hunter a bit, caught up on the by and by, and I was really happy about that. I still care for and love him very much, despite my exposition. I hope you have had a good week as well x and heading into a lovely weekend! Bless.

31st August 2020

Depop Msg: Scintalla
Margaret, would you mind if I texted you off the app?

Reply: Seralita
Hey, no probs x what's your act name if you don't mind me asking?

Depop Msg: Scintalla
My name is Deepika! pronounced deep-ick-ah

Text msgs
(+1 to +61)

31st August 2020

Deepika: Hi Margaret! it's Deepika from Depop

Seralita: Hi Deepika :) have a safe night where you are x with love from Dennis x

Deepika: He's such a baby. And lol @ the American flag pillow in the back

Margaret: He's the babiest of babies aha x it's act a literal vintage flag that I thrifted n use as a throw- I know you're not meant to use national flags as decor but it looks so impressive I'm kinda obsessed w how it comes together w the living space

Deepika: Using it as a throw is insanely good?! Is it really that comfy?

Also, like.... use the flag however you want lol no respect for the US!

And yes, the vibes are very eclectic and homey I'm here for it.

Margaret: Aha thank you x I think the USA flag carries a strong n grand visual statement tho it's act not too comfy as a throw aha it's more aesthetic than functional on my couch x

I remember having discussions w Hunter re USA/politics etc n I must admit I'm not a passionate anti-Trump/or really follow US politics or even pro-China (my ethnicity is Chinese) etc.

The way I see it, the gov is kinda there to maintain the status quo n economic/wellbeing of its citizens to ensure the country/its upper citizens remains dominant. So while on the global stage we gotta back our nation-state cos they are what define our individual freedoms/power in the world- yea on an individual level we gotta look out for ourselves rather than rely on the gov- historically no govs are at all about looking out for the most vulnerable so, yea just ensuring we apply common sense when it comes to interpreting/preparing for gov directions x

Deepika: You're absolutely right! government positions should be seen as jobs, not as a social ladder to climb up to or something that comes with "pull" and "sway". you should be held liable for your policies when they harm the public.... a lot of political ideologies are so detached from the real world even though they're made to describe and even "solve" real-world problems.

I don't think it's an issue of govt vs no govt but how to make govt about the people and not of the state.

Making the state into this omniscient, powerful entity (which is true of every almost every country and nation) is the problem.

As you said, historically, no govts look out for the vulnerable, which is why the idea of a govt has to be either reformed and eviscerated completely and replaced with a new and better "govt."

Margaret: Totally agree- ppl def go into politics bc they're drawn to the idea of wielding power/having pull- rather than for perhaps more noble reasons :(

I think what you're suggesting may involve examination and perhaps a redesign? of what governments are in essence- a system that is able to enforce social control w some sort of military mobilization to back their might. Fundamentally, govs are not representatives of ideals inequality or freedom or even the idea of serving the people- but rather exist to maintain control/order. Often maintaining order means maintaining the status quo- or in the case of revolution- establishing a new status quo. Either way (in maintaining order or in revolution) the effect of the struggle/upheaval that ensues is often at the expense of the most vulnerable/middle class/proletariat.

And for sure it would def serve to reform the concept of gov. Yet often it is at the cost of the visionaries who pioneered the reform, and it always ends up with some big wig with weird hair that gets sat in the big seat of glory in history, at least momentarily (Napoleon, Hitler, Stalin, Mao, Pol Pot... and then there are those of more recent times... aha ;).

4th September 2020

Deepika: "Big wig with weird hair" oh my god that's a historical trend I hadn't even noticed.

Also, yes, I'm defensively calling for a reform to how we see government bc the way govts have worked so far have been destructive and counterproductive (that's subjective but if you're focusing on the good of humanity, it's not lol)

***definitely not defensively

But yeah, international politics is depressing and awful, ignorance truly is bliss and knowing nothing is for the best

Also, I apologize for the late reply, this week has been awful, mentally. I feel as if I'm all over the place and nowhere at once. how have you been?

Margaret: Dam sounds like you need some rest n space for recovery x heading into the weekend soon tho n hopefully some bliss. What's been bothering you on your end? I hope it's something very temporary and that you'll find a resolution soon, perhaps w some reflection xx it's been a long one for me too, w work etc I look (and feel?) more haggard than normal aha.

Been doing a bit of writing actually, I've collated the collective listings n msgs/running comments- put it together as a running catalogue on heartbreak aha. but for real, the whole thing has been an intriguing process for sure (from July to now). Act considering putting together as a self-published book/zine (but yea mainly as a vanity project rather than for mass sale). I've done zines before, but nothing to explore a theme in this way.

Was working w the concept as the idea of engagement/interpretation to the idea of memorializing details (sometimes mundane) about a relationship. It wasn't meant to be an outpouring per se of grievances (exclusively) but a dump (atemporal) of memories and associations, to investigate how to know when something (an artwork/or a state of high emotion/distress) is complete/and the honesty/truth in memory (flexible). But always fundamentally to document and document and document x

Deepika: I adore the way you communicate, esp when it's about yourself! it's vulnerable and genuine and I admire it very much

And god I feel, heartbreak provides endless material for writing.

Margaret: That's super kind of you x n for sure, w heartbreak it shakes you up on a deeply personal level x but always remember to stay true. Time is long and moments (happy or not) are always changing.

Deepika: The zine sounds fascinating!

I barely know what a zine is but I've heard people talk about it.

Margaret: Aha basically a booklet of self-published copy/ in prose or lyrical form w images - a bunch of music/expressively inclined made loads in the 90s I think but yea just basically self-published self-made packages of text n image.

Deepika: And yes! Crazy how you memorize so many things in a relationship? I remember his birthday, his phone number, the day we hooked up, etc etc.

!! a zine sounds like a great idea! if u made one I'd most likely get it if it's affordable.

Margaret: The person/their character/istics don't stop being significant just because the relationship is ending- for me this is. I know that yea there's that whole go kick rocks, find someone who can love me at my worst deserve me at my best, bye boy etc mentality of self-empowerment too- n sure if that is something that feels right, I think it's probably a personal match. He meant/s a lot to me. N yea those details don't evaporate n lose significance x

And thank you so much for your support!! May I list you in the acknowledgements section? perhaps by your depop handle? I'm going to try n get a digital version out on kindle not sure how but will knuckle it out aha xx the price I'm going to make prob his birthday $21.09 AUD (XXxx Xxx- Virgo) ha.

Or whatever number holds more auspicious symbolism

Deepika: I'm in a great relationship now but I still think about him and how awful that relationship was.

And yes please do! u can use 'deepika' if you'd like

Margaret: Thank you x and I'm so happy to hear that you are in a joyful place now

Deepika: <Screenshot 1,2>

Deepika: This is something I wrote a year ago when I was a lot closer to the situation.

This is my first real relationship (the one I'm in now) so it's challenging but ultimately fulfilling to be with someone who wants me.

And respects me.

Margaret: This is beautiful.

Deepika: It's the only thing I wrote about him I haven't deleted bc like you said, it lasts forever.

I deleted everything in hopes I'll forget but I think this was more about me than him.

And thank you, that means a lot coming from you

Margaret: I understand that completely. Try to hold on to the sweetness, until maybe it fades. I don't feel at this point in time that it will. But maybe it will be something new and with new potential in future. Thank you so much for sharing your writing with me. It is deeply personal, and I appreciate so much that you chose to share the glimpse into you.

have a happy and safe weekend as it comes x sending love

Deepika: Thank you for the kind feedback- sometimes I feel guilty for thinking about the past, esp bc my man is the 'move on with no regrets' type.

And please!! I hope your weekend is restful and kind to you!

Margaret: Everyone has their individual philosophy/mentality and it's really what works for you at the end of the day. My parents are the complete opposite of me in their no-nonsense approach to sentimentality (they aren't sentimental lol) and that has worked well for them in life. But yea we gotta do what's necessary to make it work x sleep tight.

6th September 2020

Deepika: Not to be nosy! but what's your sun sign? do you have your birth chart by chance?

Margaret: Hey not at all aha I don't know my sun sign or birth chart tho :s my bday's Xxx Xxx XXXX, I know I'm a Scorpio :) hbu x

Deepika: Scorpio is your sun sign! I'm a cancer sun
https://astromatrix.app/#/intro?report=%2Fbirth
This site would give u information! My birthday is Xxxx XX,XXXX

Margaret: Sweet thank you x

18th September 2020

Deepika: Margaret, what do you read? Who're your favorite authors?

Margaret: Hey Deepika ! I don't know if I have a specific genre :) I have really enjoyed A Lovers Discourse by Barthes, the Master and Margarita (aha), and the unbearable lightness of being xx all three I gushed to Hunter who's also incredibly well-read (more so than I am!!)

Hbu?

Hope you're going well! It's been a busy week on my end xx n I've dropped off the deep end in contact sorry but still going strong

Deepika: I've never heard of those but I'll check them out! It feels like I've been bombarded with philosophy lately. Whether it's reading books, conversations or even just my own thoughts. It feels a bit like drowning? I just want to be shallow and spend a lot of $$$ to balance the scale lol

And I'm doing well, thank you! How have you been? and no worries lol you're very busy and this is my last semester at uni so I've been consistently occupied with one thing or another

Margaret: For sure get the feeling!!! Ahaha nothing like something gratifying on the short n up thru retail xo I'm glad you're doing well!! Can only imagine it's getting real at this time of the year w assessments/submissions xx it's Hunters bday coming up, I act did my annual tradition now aha of getting him a bunch of stuff ;) it makes me happy to know he's happy, we're a bit better now, as um friends x been busy w work really, n yea looking into editing my stuff n ways of publication.

 (Btw your writing is incredible, keep keep keep what you've written n keep writing x)

Deepika: It feels like my life is solidifying and I can't do anything about it. I'm so used to everything being in flux so this is all a bit terrifying.

I'm really happy that you're doing well with Hunter!! And it's nice to hear that your research is coming along nicely and you're doing well overall

And thank you so much, it really means a lot to hear that from you like I can't express in words how lovely it is to read that.

Margaret: Mmmm have you ever read the bell jar by Plath? x

I think I could relate to that feeling. Many options but perhaps nothing that stands out among them as the truest, and so it's just a sea of possibility and perhaps the choice of one means the extinguishing of all the others? I dunno if people truly are clear in their personal directions.. I know that I'm not. I spoke on this to Hunter before, like outside of having trustworthy guidance n support to break down or analyze the options, sometimes it's just about gunning it and making that (considered- rather than heedless) choice. Bc once you've started so the way, you'll naturally start to learn n resolve everything that comes up, and make adjustments as needed. But it's just about taking that step forward x

Started on the way*

And thank you x

Deepika: I have read it, but it was ages ago. And yeah, what you said about being not clear in personal directions really resonates. I keep thinking of all the alternate realities and what could've been and I don't know how to get rid of this mentality. I think this just ties into my curious nature—one can't choose what they're curious about, you know? So maybe the point isn't to get rid of this bc it would go against something innate but try to get around it somehow.

And yes! the last two sentences sound a lot like "trust the process" but better lol, life truly is about solving problems one after the other as they crop up.

Margaret: Sometimes making one decision doesn't exclude the others, but maybe brings you closer to them, perhaps over time or in unexpected ways. When I changed from being a fine art/philosophy student to study traditional Chinese medicine, for sure I felt a sense of reluctance bc it was seemingly moving away from my identity towards science n research (def not my strength or my interest per se). But yeah you make these disciplines/what you learn work for You, not the other way around- instead of somehow being limited by them. I mean sure you are moulded by what you choose to surround yourself with. But it's your mentality that guides who you become, and how things feed that process. If that makes sense..

And ahaha trust in the process~ Hunter as a Virgo is super indecisive, and I said those words to urge him to action to make a decision. Bc once you have started, you will be compelled to make those corollary adjustments where needed to sort it all out/or make changes as necessary. But you don't know until you begin. x

*To clarify, TCM is my interest for sure but yea I'm not big on science or research is what I meant x

Hunter is smart when it comes to that stuff and w maths. Not me tho...

Deepika: It does make sense and when I think about, everything boils down to the inane amount of fear I have in my life. I feel defeated and afraid of new opportunities and the unknown. Everything is scary for no good reason. I think it was the way I was raised, to be afraid and cautious of things but it's a hard shell to step out of.

Maybe I depend too much on my emotions entirely? looking for something that "feels right" or not opting for opportunities bc I don't "feel" that I'm fully on board. Where's the line between feelings and intuition? Do you listen to either? Frankly, I hate when logic is placed above emotions; I understand that's necessary depending on the situation but those who insist on science and logic all the time are the same people who aren't in control of their feelings and don't know how to handle or react to their emotions, even if they're grown.

And god I feel that I'm not good with math either.....it's a headache.

Margaret: Be brave. It's necessary to be careful, and it's great if you got familial support to back you. It's difficult to step out of what is familiar. It's what I kinda am grateful to Hunter for, inspiring me to desire more than what is safe and familiar to me. The world is big and time is long, and yea opportunities as whether we recognize what they are n act on them/are in a position to. Always dare (within reason ;) the more you do the more courage you'll gain as you accrue more ability that comes w experience xx

I'm a fairly emotional person lol can prob tell by how I conduct my shop aha but yea nothing can actually bring you down unless you let it, nothing external that is unless you let it in. Nothing wrong w being emotional I think... it's probably a more honest way of living rather than using logic to rationalize a situation ad infinitum until all responsibility is rationalized into vapor aha but yea that's my take xx

So build your capacity n exercise your ability xxx you'll be stronger to take on whatever comes your way.

21st September 2020

Deepika: I think you're right, about being brave and not letting things get to you. I've always absorbed everything around me bc I wasn't interested in being somebody with a stubborn and fixed personality who doesn't learn from others and change their thinking when new information arises. I think I absorbed the bad stuff to a point where everything was my fault even if it wasn't? Like I'd be trying to set boundaries and if it isn't received well or the other person takes offense I'd immediately start thinking that I was in the wrong. It took me a long time to start showing up and standing by the decisions I made (I literally just started doing this yesterday). But yeah thank u for your insight, it's always lovely to hear your sage advice haha. I think it's Monday for you down there in Aus so I hope the rest of your week is wonderful!

Also! just saw that you liked Thomas Mann back in hs, what a coincidence! I started reading a collection of his short stories a while back. I surprisingly enjoy his writing; it's pretentious at times but entertaining.

Margaret: Hope you're having a great end to the weekend! It's Hunter's bday today aha he's not here w me but yea, my heart is always w him

Mmm I feel like I'm the opposite to what you've described !! as the very stubborn fixed personality who only very reluctantly changes n doesn't take a hint Teflon resilient to the advice of others aha I'm being hyperbolic but I do gotta learn to be as you've described :) as more open to change. Maybe my innate personality coupled w my upbringing, I grew up with my identity n interests being described as having poor/low value, and rather than assert myself, I instead hid away inside me my true thoughts and sentiments, and would instead present as compliant, meanwhile straight-up rejecting it all (advice, information- tho both were often shared w an agenda) in my heart. It's taken some time for me to learn to face things head-on.

You are too funny. Right here, def FAR from sage aha.

It's important to set boundaries tho. Apparently, I keep overstepping Hunter's... sorry. It's prob more important to be clear w yourself in knowing what is acceptable n what's not. I'm turning 30 in nov. way too old to be caring about whether I've stepped on toes or if my xyz is fashionable, popular, whether close friends or strangers will easily accept me - I dunno the stuff I would dwell on when I was younger, how I came off etc etc. not saying to be a loose cannon/have zero self-awareness, but yea, everyone's got finite time and I don't got time for that aha.

Aha I love how you also read TM! And Agreed! His writing came off as a bit erudite n I loved it for that quality aha x trying to yea just part w the books on depop. I dunno if I wanna be amassing all the books I've read as a literary graveyard in my home lol on a bookcase, just have a few that I keep returning to, but yea into the wild w the rest xxx

23rd September 2020

Deepika: Sage advice = valuable viewpoint!! it's nice to talk to/with you, there's an air of lightness because you're never actually advising or directing but sharing your experiences and how you felt/saw something which I guess is what a conversation is but I don't know, airy conversations are rare lately. everything feels heavy, like wet cotton haha.

Your personality seems more fluid and adaptable than described but maybe my (over-) sensitivity can be traced back to my childhood too I think. My therapist once mentioned something about being sensitized to hurt and that statement felt like a betrayal because I didn't choose to exist like that, it was kind of just thrust upon me? maybe I take things too personally and that's my entire problem who's to say.

And how are things with Hunter? Is it hard to be close to him but also far? the whole caring less about things as you get older makes sense but do you think it applies to people like Hunter, who you have a history with or just strangers, acquaintances, etc? I think "caring less" is more like shedding unnecessary anxiety like when you'd step into a crowded room or public space and immediately feel people's eyes on you and feel small, shy and anxious. I think you get more comfortable with the world and yourself as time goes on so that's always something to look forward to, I guess.

And I wish I could buy your zines and books but I live all the way across the world!

Margaret: I like how you describe things, I feel like sometimes there's a dreamy quality to your metaphors which I find redolent of some of Murakami's earlier writing? (I haven't read his more recent). And thank you I enjoy msging w you/talking to you too! and yea it's I guess an unconventional experience n connection, but one that I'm v grateful to have found xx

I don't know, it's like our past experiences rough us up and add scales/cynicism to our armor, naturally, as a self defense mechanism to prevent re-injury, but yeah sometimes it is wayyy off, so much that it fucks w the clarity of our perception. Being sensitized to it would suggest a previous injury that hasn't quite recovered or has perhaps overlaid in the recovery process, a scar that may under circumstances still reflect those past sensations?? :(

I was told once by a therapist that rather than react (as I'm prone and wont to aha) to instead hold on and wait, to take a step back and consider over some time - rather than explode/be overwhelmed in the emotional moment. And often yea whatever that reaction was (perhaps one of anxiety or bristling with injustice aha) it becomes less inflamed after that moment of consideration has passed.

It is a taxing life to often take on criticism/approval of others to heart. It may be a cynical viewpoint, but I find that few people are genuinely happy for my own personal success.

Perhaps bc they don't benefit from this...?

Correspondingly, I care less for unsolicited commentary/judgement from others- again not to say it's all my way or the high way- just I try to be more discerning, and clear in knowing that my decisions are towards building my own life - which is separate from theirs.

And that's why I do care a lot for what Hunter thinks of me. Bc I love him lol. But also bc I want to eventually share a life with him. To have shared goals/be united.
I thought/think of him as family. Like for real adopted that 'we' mentality that couples migrated into aha.

I won't change myself for him or want him to change. I only want to better myself to keep that possibility alive and the potential for that possible reality.

For me at least, I have noticed among my friends, that people may front a show of concern/solidarity- but what indeed drives their interest is not true care but voyeurism, and perhaps a sense of delight or relief in what is perceived as unhappiness and drama.

Maybe it more speaks of the quality of some of my friendships.. aha :(((

Strangely, some of my friendships suddenly came to life during my rough times with Hunter- and then just as abruptly fizzled out when they realized that he and I were on the mend.

I didn't reach out during those downtimes. But got hit up. And when he n I were on the up, I got again hit up with similarly unsolicited expressions of (always well-meaning) disapproval?? telling me that I was w him for superficial reasons- for his looks (I'm not/it's not) or telling me he is using me and suggesting that I was mentally limited by my affection for him and thus blind to this supposed fact.

I dunno. I mean sure, maybe they think they're being well-meaning. But I gotta make decisions for myself- what's gonna work out best for my life- what I can accept. Only I can make the call on that. N I've learned to separate those external voices I guess.

I guess yea, that's what I meant about caring less. And also, just noting that we're all born worthy- no more no less- and After that, we make who we are. We all got the same amount of sky above us and earth beneath us. No one can really belittle that truth away.
N thank you for your support- I gotta work out digital copies for zines !!! Still on the editing for the book/manuscript - experimenting with it a bit formally will def hit you up when/if yea it gets anywhere ! xx

27th Septemeber 2020

Deepika: I've never read Murakami but I will check him out! And yes, omg, I think you're right about past scars not being healed all the way bc why else would it be sensitive?

Good, solid friendships are so hard to find and keep. Even harder than relationships maybe bc monogamy is applied to relationships but not to friendships so people just come and in and out of your life and that's just how it is. Not that toxic is the opposite of "good" friendships but just something that lasts? Is so hard to find with friendships :(it's genuinely crazy that your friends cross your boundaries like that and get involved in your relationship.....it's so disrespectful.

And yes!! I'd love to be updated on the zine/whatever you're working on!

And sorry for the late reply! been busy with school and life as usual

Margaret: His writing is very accessible but the style carries an- imo- understated poetry you might like it? I'm not sure what kinda books you're into xx what are some of your go to's?

And yeah for sure w the scars. I was watching a YouTube of Iliza Shlesinger's stand up; she did this impression of a woman walking the collective baggage from all past relationships into the next aha it was pretty spot on. But yea, it's exhausting to live that way, be burdened I suppose w past disappointments or be holding onto unhappiness in that way. I'm not one to speak tho aha.

I agree with you deadass "good, solid friendships are hard to find and keep." Notwithstanding that people have their own agendas/insecurities/jealousies. Even friendships that were once close- everyone changes over time and yeah if it was a bunch of interests that once held you together, those transform over time passed, and - for me at least- it becomes an increasing battle to maintain the once-intimacy.

I dunno tho, Hunter makes friends on the go and quickly- it probably speaks more abt his personality (open and generous and kind) and reflects on mine (more closed, reserved, and umm w spice). But I dunno, I would hesitate to say those are true friends of his, but rather people coming together temporarily for an aligned purpose. I would sometimes rankle at the thought of him maybe considering those friendships as more 'real' than I saw them as/perhaps were. But perhaps that's the nature of all friendships? A very pragmatic and in-the-present give and take? I guess that idea depresses me, bc I am probably a bit romantic. I get too caught up trying to discern whether the friendship/love/relationship is 'true'/'real'… and yeah it would probably be better to be more easy-going x

And no need to apologize x it's really lovely msging w you n for sure will keep you in the loop re the writing xxx

28th September 2020

Deepika: I like the 48 laws of power by Robert Greene but it's about to be 2 years since I've got it and I still haven't finished it!! I loved The Catcher in the Rye bc I related heavily to Holden Caulfield when I was 16....lmao. I don't own many books of my own bc I don't read most books more than once? I prefer going to the library. Three women by Lisa Taddeo was one I read recently and it was SO good. The epub is available on lib gen, if you want. I also really like Susan Sontag, Anne Carson (I think I've only read quotes by her....never a full work tho I'm a poser :/), Adrienne Rich, Nizar Qabbani, Octavio Paz, A handbook of disappointed fate by Anne Boyer (there's this section called erotology that you would love and find heavily relatable I think, the pdf of the whole book should be available on lib gen too) tonio Kroger by Thomas Mann (I enjoyed Mario the magician by him too). My boyfriend loaned me his copy of widow basquiat and it was heartbreaking and well-written :(I'm also reading his copy of letters from a stoic by Seneca and marking like, every other page lol.

Yeah, I was about to say, I don't think the friendships Hunter makes are real bc I've made a lot of wonderful, short-term friendships and they were great! But short term. And in most situations, neither person is to blame....life just happens. I think most relationships are more about people getting along instead of the individuals themselves.

Growing up, I learned to value my friendships over my family simply bc I didn't want to value my family members.

....I wanted a different option you know? I wanted to choose my relationships for myself. And almost all my friendships have been rewarding when I look back on it, even if they were also disappointing. It's just weird to see people who've been friends since childhood bc I don't have that lol. I don't even know what that's like, which is crazy. My man has friends and exes all over the world and he didn't have anybody he considered a real, true friend (versus those "quick friendships" u mentioned) in America until he met me. And he knows tons of people here and they're wonderful people but he doesn't get along with them in that deep, treasured manner we all want from our true, long-lasting friendships. And I felt the same way about him; I'd had friends I'd known for a long time but never considered anybody my best friend until I met him. He's my significant other now and it's better, but I wish I had a best friend again. Lol. I sound spoiled.

And I've written a ton already sorry for making you read thru so much but I think all relationships, regardless of the degree of intimacy and closeness, are true and real simply bc they exist. They have no choice but to be real, you know? Unless somebody has ulterior motives or is using you.

Disappointing, ephemeral friendships can be true, real, valuable and not enough all at the same time. That's what makes life so sick sometimes—the irony. Like "this is great! but I want more." I think being more "easygoing" is realizing this fact along the way and learning to live with it. Or sigh and keep moving forward every time you lose a friend.....hopefully there's less sighing in the future than there has been in the past lol.

29th September 2020

Margaret: Ah it is now my time to apologize to you for the lapse in response, sorry I've just been a bit down and preoccupied in trying to edit/put together the text. I guess the main reason for the low mood is bc I don't know rn how supportive Hunter is about me doing this. It's all first world problems aha- but I don't think that makes them any less relevant, it's all I guess in how we handle them.

I don't know. It blows hot and cold with him and tbh it confuses me when at points he stops responding to me- and then when he does it feels as though he is frustrated with me, and this all makes me uncertain (again) of where I stand with him. I've always wanted to feel close to him, and we are until he pushes me away again, seemingly (to me at least) without reason. I've been very transparent to him on where I stand, which has tbh never really changed. Sometimes I feel very alone in this as certainly no one within my immediate family (not that their opinion on these matters really means much!!) or my close friends are v supportive or actually understand the relationship. So when he himself pushes me away, I don't know. I begin to really wonder what is the point to any of it, and this makes me paralyzed with unhappiness and uncertainty.

I've never desired to be partnered with anyone, in truth, before I met him. I was prepared to be a spinster for life aha, devoted to art and couture-related consumerism aha. But I guess I've always yearned, perhaps as we all do? for that unique person to be understood by. As I feel that he does and to that unparalleled depth.

You've read some incredible books! I love catcher in the rye!! Holden Caulfield and the great gatsby were what really got me interested in literature (it was grade 9 English class!! aha).

I gotta check out what you've mentioned!! Super pumped :) And ooh just noting that Hunter has also read Seneca! I think, he's read in and identifies w stoicism- too much imo aha.

You sound like you have an incredible relationship rn. It's rare I think to find a true/deep connection w someone, and what you describe sounds like something to be treasured. I think you are right and very wise to recognize that "disappointing, ephemeral friendships can be true, real, valuable and not enough at the same time." I don't think I have the courage sometimes to reconcile with that totality, and instead relegate those experiences as 'not true' to be able to devalue them in my mind and not experience the disappointment in finding that they indeed have ended and passed. But oftentimes, for me at least, I do note a transactional trend to those relationships (within both family and friends).

I'm looking for something that lasts forever. Prob bc I have never truly experienced this unconditionally, and the romantic side of me yearns for this. But perhaps nothing does stay forever.

I however, would like to buck that trend. Prob bc I am stubborn like Hunter once suggested I'm prepared to stay forever waiting for him, even if he never comes back to me. This is not to be encouraged... but it makes sense to me, bc I see it as a true expression of the sentiment that I feel. Even if it is ummm somewhat sad ?? (Miss Havisham?? Aha). I just want to remain loyal to that, even yea... if it means a lifetime spent in dust and untouched by the sun...

I understand what you mean wishing to have a best friend again. I've always had bfs historically (and the relationships have always been v intimate) but they've since ended amicably/acrimoniously/sometimes dramatically haha. I really value those connections, the close unfiltered ones where you feel safe to be open and feel real intimacy with. Sometimes I feel that they can only truly be with your partner, bc ultimately they are the one (maybe?) that you will build a future/and life with. That united goal towards something, n that commitment, while all other relationships will invariably be prised away by the exigencies of life.

3rd October 2020

Deepika: I am so sorry for not answering soon!! This week feels like there were several weeks inside it so much going on.

I don't mean to pass judgment (definitely not one to do that lol) but your relationship with Hunter seems so stressful. It reminds me of my time with Xxxx (before my current bf). Xxxx and I were never in a formal relationship bc I never let it get that far but I used to feel the same way about him: like he's so special and wonderful and all that. I think I still do on some level but at the same time, I don't understand it? Lol. He's a very insecure, immature, lonely, self-absorbed person and everybody around him can see it (I've heard from mutual friends who don't know that he and I had a thing) so I just feel confused? That I ever felt this way about him. It was probably bc he was the first person I was truly intimate with (not just sex-wise), he would make me breakfast, talk late with me etc and I guess that left a lasting impression on me, even if the person wasn't that great

Definitely don't mean to compare our relationships though, that's disrespectful, I only meant that I can relate. (And dw about replying quickly, I don't mind at all!!) I think you're right that nothing lasts forever but there's peace to be found there instead of worrying when something might end. Every time something bad happened, I thought "nothing good will ever happen again." But good things kept happening. And bad thing's happened too. And it just kept going. There was no point in keeping track of it all, when it was very arbitrary, these good and bad things that kept happening. And as strange as it sounds, the arbitrary quality is what provides experiences meaning? Bc you don't have to worry about controlling anything, you're just here to experience. You're small, but that's okay bc you're allowed to be small.

And I forgot to add great expectations to my list of reads but I read that recently and it was good! I actually enjoyed the weaving plot. And miss Havisham....is a character. Interesting to see you've embraced her wholeheartedly bc most people wouldn't (besides, you're so complex and wonderful whereas Havisham is so...simple(-minded?) but maybe you both have that same certain stubbornness when it comes to matters of the heart).

I've always valued my friendships but truly.....no one is ever going to know an individual like their significant other does. And that's not meant to be taken in a romantic sense necessarily bc the things people reveal about themselves for the sake of vulnerability and intimacy are terrifying. They'll say the most horrifying things out loud because all they want is to be accepted, like the rest of us. It scares me in a way, bc you have to get that close to a person to know them bc I don't want to get close to every single person I come across but living without knowing people's true intentions towards the world and others is also not an option for me. I guess that's why I strive to be so perceptive and inquisitive? I have to know everything lol.

I knew this guy who had done something...not good years ago and his intentions, thoughts, opinions about that thing he'd done betrayed guilt but more like....he felt bad he'd been caught and received consequences, not bad that he'd done something that had hurt other people. I didn't realize this at first bc he expressed regret but when someone changes, they change as a whole, and all parts of them are affected, not just the part they're trying to fix. Anyway, the way this guy spoke about the thing he had done, and connected subjects showed that he hadn't changed at all but acted and expressed "change" or rather, the "effort" it takes to change. And the only reason I knew all this and could tell the difference was bc he was exposing himself to be as a potential SO and he wanted to be accepted. He really thought being with me would've "absolved" and "forgiven" him bc he was in a loving healthy relationship and only good people deserve that. He literally called me his (only?) source of serotonin lmao he was a joke.

But yeah lmao that's what I'm talking when I say no one can know anybody the way their SO knows them bc this dude would have NEVER told his friends the things he'd told me and they all thought he was this amazing, progressive feminist or whatever.

(But he wasn't)

Margaret: Hey you don't need to apologize to me about the length of text xx esp given my proclivity to go off at length aha! I hope you're having a chance to wind down now over the weekend xx

How good is the great expectations!! Aha MH is difficult to sympathize w. You're right it's not her character arc that I largely identify w, but rather what I read into her - the character's potential for undying dedication- which is clearly NOT expressed in the narrative aha.

At the same time tho, I do vibe with the idea of vengeance (a theme that's also explored in Medea). The enactment of wrath and the (warped?) perception of justice delivered by the woman scorned- it's always kinda held my imagination as something incredibly satisfying.

In past moments when I have taken up this mantle (spitefully but also ironically) - it has been gratifying without parallel lol. The acts themselves tho didn't carry the same heavy emotional weight tho bc I didn't love/care feel for these men, but were instead encouraged by the objective injustice of the respective situations, which I felt were a perfect setting against which I could plot and carry out these almost theatrical mini acts of revenge (nothing as comparably dire of course!) and always w relish n gusto- sometimes in a tag team effort w my gfs. I enjoyed the drama, and the chance to pay back some of these admittedly piggish guys, some of whom are similar to those that you've described, who would pay lip service to being progressive/feminist and identify w whatever is the zeitgeist on-trend- in order to gain social capital to charm other boys n girls.

I dunno, I've always kept a keen radar for pretentious (untrue) guys- whether their exclusivity is their music, ideas, money, career, etc, there's just something repugnant about that mentality and to the idea that they could dangle an (oftentimes illusory) carrot in the hopes of winning me, charming me, fooling me, buying me. Yea gross. In dating them, as I sometimes would (for the novelty? the anthropological experience? bc they were cute? I don't know, maybe bc I was curious- aren't we all?), I stepped into a role, as when I had a dancer, and Became the girl they thought I was, that they were trying to impress. I guess I've never been truly authentic w guys prior to H. Sure there were moments of intimacy but I would quickly extinguish these bc I knew that I couldn't afford to be authentic when I knew that they were innately untrue in their intentions/actions w me.

I think people will always judge us, even the right guy/girl. Judgement is inescapable but it's just a matter of extent/the place the judgement comes from. N it's terrifying to be privy to these darker glimpses of whatever underbelly of confession shared during moments of intimacy, or to divulge them at the risk of being reviled/ridiculed/judged/viewed henceforth differently.

I judged Hunter, constantly appraised him- bc I wanted to know who he is what he was about - in order to determine whether I needed to protect myself from that and to what extent. I still judge him, but probably? no more than what I would apply to myself, in hopes of being constructive, positive? I dunno, maybe he feels differently and thinks that I'm constantly on his case :s I'm not trying to be..

That guy you spoke of, who described you as being his serotonin? (I'm being judgey now pls pardon me) He sounds rather selfish and insecure if he is looking for absolution/atonement for whatever crimes thru achieving a relationship rather than being genuine to the experience of that relationship in all its idiosyncrasies. Perhaps he thought that in being w someone like you (unique?discerning? intelligent/intellectual? curious and inquisitive) it would confer upon him by the grace of your selection of him: worthiness. I mean that thought is both flattering in a sense and v reductive, and kinda reflects a certain insecurity in him. Maybe he is staunch in other qualities, but perhaps in time, he'll approach relationships w more maturity...

It definitely isn't easy trying to maintain a relationship with Hunter. He's never been in a relationship before. Sometimes I think he's still a kid at heart. Bc his actions (I mean in particular those actions that hurt me) are not calculated, I eventually look past those moments, and return to a feeling of fondness for him- a concession that I've never afforded others before him, in either love or friendship.

It's not a battered-wife mentality I swear (and I use this concept figuratively- he's not at all violent) the 'oh he didn't intend it- so it's all good' slippery slope. I let it slide bc I believe in him, and also I am secure in who I am, and like who I am- as before I met him, now, and in moments without him- n trust in my judgement. Mmmm it sounds achingly similar to battered-wife logic- but yea I dunno, that's a grand concept- and many situations are more nuanced, n come down to how we handle them and practice acceptance/and at times tolerance for those with whom we enter into a unity.

I perceive a sincere naivety in Hunter's open-hearted approach to life, to friendships, and in that simplicity (I don't mean this pejoratively- but rather that it is pared back and organic, uncomplicated, and not polluted by ulterior motives) I interpret a certain purity, and goodness. It is true; I do adore him, for his intelligence and character traits. I do think he is wonderful- but I'm also very aware of the less-than-perfection of his numerous foibles- that I won't bore us both by listing aha- but they sure do annoy the Fuck out of me.

Hunter isn't the first or only man I was intimate w either emotionally or physically. As I said, he is the only one that I saw fit to be indeed honest and authentic with, and I gave myself to him in complete openness and sincerity. I'm reluctant to let this/him go, bc I guess I interpret the relationship as something uniquely elevated, and that we have a really strong potential, and a life with him would be incredible.

Even if it is not so, I don't want to betray its memory or seek to replace it. I dunno if I'm wasting my life, shunning opportunities. I don't want to be hurtling forward in the hustle of 'moving on' and towards the endless possibilities that I feel is the vogue in the modern mentality. I want to make a (measured) sacrifice to see it through adversity, to investigate if it is indeed 'worthwhile,' which in itself is a summative idea that can't be clearly known except in time.

I know that Hunter's just acting/reacting in the moment to stressers that he doesn't know how to handle (aka me aha). And yea similar to how you described your relationship w Xxxx, Hunter and I were never in a formal relationship. I was always homegirl to him- however, in terms of the level of intimacy between us and the actions this has inspired, it would be ungenerous (and inaccurate) for it to be described as anything less.

I think Hunter is reluctant to place labels, and tbh I don't feel like I'm particularly pedantic when it comes to titles and labels- and never really impressed on him for us to 'be' something. It is important for me, however, that he/this remains meaningful, which to me means contact to maintain an experience of intimacy. I am (stubbornly and relentlessly) loyal to that- although not necessarily faithfully. And I'm okay if he's with other people (don't love it tho- and get super mad when he tells me about it). I want him to keep me in his heart, in the hope that he may perhaps one day come back to me if he wants to, when he is ready.

4th October 2020

Deepika: Yes!! Miss Havisham definitely reminded me of revenge but I didn't want to say it out loud in case it offended you! Her plan with estella and pip was perfect, cruel, elegant and very...invested, shall we say. Not at all shallow. Something only a woman could've thought of. I think vengeance solely and rightfully belongs to women.

And god, I wish I could get back at some of the men I've known and been with. But karma really is a thing and it's funny how it works. I know that should make me feel better but I'd rather have a hand in my payback instead of it being automatically "just" in terms of the universe or whatever. I guess I want to play god? Lol call me a megalomaniac.

From what you said, it seems like you appraise all of your SOs? (Again not meant to be judge-y I apologize if it comes off that way!!) that must be very hard on you—Do you ever feel wish you could be yourself with them? Just have the freedom to lower your guard and enjoy the moment instead of looking out for the wool to be pulled over your eyes? I want to say that it's the nature of men to be cowardly and dishonest with their intentions but I fear of sounding like a man-hater (I don't care too much for the title but I don't really believe in the actual responsibility that comes with the role). Idk I think if men were slightly trustworthy as an entire subspecies, everything would be a lot easier.

And yes! You are right to describe the guy who called me serotonin as immature and insecure! Absolutely! He was pathetic! That sounds cruel but the lack of self-awareness was truly astounding. I have no respect for somebody like that. He was trying to own me/the idea of me as his SO the entire time we were "together". But not in a hot "She's my property don't touch her" possessive manner, more like a shield against the world. He wasn't somebody I'd like to be owned by. I found myself mothering him at some points and I was truly disgusted with myself and him. He literally cried once over the phone to me telling me that I had no idea how hard it is to be a man- I hate men lol (idk if saying that qualifies me as a man-hater??? I just love saying those precious three words—they have a lovely ring to them).

I think I understand. My bf isn't perfect and he can be insensitive and frustrating sometimes, esp when it comes to emotions but I can never be truly mad/angry with him bc he's so genuine. When I tell him he's hurt or me or I need him to change him, he expressed regret and he really does try to change, which is nice. He does it for himself, not just for me, you know? It's hard to explain this to my friends sometimes bc it makes him seem like a bad guy but he's not, he just makes mistakes and no relationship is perfect 100% of the time. I definitely don't think you're like the battered-wife or even a victim. Hunter may have hurt you a lot and that's on him. Your decision to love him and keep him around is yours, and even if it's not the best decision (as everyone around you seems to think, from your texts) I think people should respect that you're doing what's best for you? You're emotionally intelligent, considerate and GROWN lol. you can stand by your decisions without needing to explain yourself. I love that about you—you're very strong but in an independent, vulnerable way. It's not a desperate, impulsive "strength" that runs on adrenaline and impulse.

I sincerely apologize if any of this comes off as judgmental, that is genuinely not my intention! I really love that we get to talk about this and delve deep into these subjects and I don't want to violate your trust/boundaries/etc.

And it's crazy that you and Hunter were never in a formal relationship but you were (almost?) engaged? that sounds like a rollercoaster.

And ofc your time as a dancer, you've truly lived a storied and interesting life.

5th October 2020

Margaret: Aha please don't worry about pulling back from offending me and thanks for being kind n considerate n for checking in w me- n def nothing to be apologetic for!

I certainly find the idea of vengeance attractive! Maybe bc I'm a bitch! aha I'm joking, but in circumstances I can be. Something in the concept of vengeance implies that it is in some sense justified/or deserved, a means to correct some miscarriage of justice. And i guess there's a sense of empowerment to be able to take up that mantle and personally deliver the blow- a satisfaction in delivering that restoration of supposed justice. Indeed I agree that women are capable of harnessing deliciously cruel imaginations, to devise deviously considered and grippingly ironic plots, and conduct them with mastery and elegance. It is... a lot of work. Every act carries its own set of karma, including the act of vengeance itself. And I guess it's to be judged per situation: to weigh up the satisfaction of taking it into your own hands, against the cost/burden on your time, mental space (all of which could be invested in more constructive/positive? -in a general sense- directions, more aligned w your life interests, rather than wasting even more life on someone/thing clearly unworthy)- as well as of course the risk of its impact in potentially poisoning your own character.

I personally like to have a bit of fun with it, and determine whether to go that way on a case to case basis aha.

You are right in saying that it is a hard/tiring way to live to be constantly appraising people, particularly potential SOs of their intentions/agendas. I guess I mean that I try to be extra discerning in the early stages of knowing someone, with the idea of saving myself the trouble down the line. Bc I accepted who I recognized they are from the start.

I don't know where this particularly pointed wariness stems from, but I guess I don't trust people (men in particular, but also women) easily, and it's more about self-protection. I'm def more reserved compared to Hunter who receives people with more openness. So to that effect, in the initial moments of getting to know men, I deliberately investigate their responses to me and to the various 'challenges' that I throw up to try to provoke/get a glimpse of who they are beneath any potential artifice. To see how they would handle being contradicted, to see how they would react; are they generous of spirit or are they more guarded- and ultimately can I accept this collective of characteristics.

It's not formulaic, like a set of things that I ask or a certain way I behave, although I do have certain favored topics that invite a bit more spice. I guess I'm trying to pick up signs of inauthenticity, and desire to investigate any possible underlying agendas. And where the intention is not in line with what I considered honorable, im quick to shut down that connection from becoming emotionally closer.

I do this particularly with guys in a manner that I Hope is playful and w good humor, rather than condescending or clinical. I am purposive in collecting what I consider vital information for this decision making process.

I don't keep scrutinizing people though afterwards. Sure I still judge Hunter n closer friends, as I would prob judge myself, to try and find improvements, understand limitations, but not in the sense that I'm picking them apart and keeping count and analyzing stuff on the constant on some sort of seesaw-scale or balance.

Although I don't hate men, I totally vibe w the term man-hater aha. Once upon a time my gfs and I started a literary and lingerie group (it didn't take off aha) called the Diced Dick - where essentially the three of us would share different artistic/classical textual or image references of this sentiment amongst one another, while we designed different bras and panties- which never really made it past looking at fabric samples. Ahahaha. Good times.

Guys similar to the one you've described are unfortunately in no shortage, possibly worldwide. Their behaviors can be quite revolting.. I try to be quick in seeing these guys for what they are early on...

In how you've described your current relationship, it sounds very solid. I think you're right that it comes down to the genuineness of the desire to make improvements. It's not about making changes for someone else, to please/appease them. Individuals should want to be refining themselves for the better, and it's a test of character/indicative of a certain maturity to be able to accept criticism and face whatever it means to take it on. It's difficult to face our own shortcomings.

In a relationship you're in something together, facing things as a team bc the consequences and the outcome are shared- or they should be in the sense that you share a direction (as separate individuals of course).

The relation between Hunter and I is undefined and always was (bc he didn't want to define it). Amongst my friends and colleagues, he was affectionately known as my future husband aha. It's an in-joke, a reference to my ardent desire to be with him and also to his suggestion of this possibility for matrimony at one point in time.

He was a bit inconsistent in being able to accept what we are bc he isnt certain about what he wants and is reluctant to bring me along for a ride that could ultimately be very disappointing if the outcome diverged from a promise made at the outset. So he made none. It's not cowardice, I think he is trying to be honorable, to refuse to say something only to take it back or to make wild promises with reckless abandon simply bc it would make it easier in the moment.

I'm not wildly trying to hustle him down the aisle- never really cared about that. I have considered the benefits and costs of being w him, in marriage or not is irrelevant, and it is my hope, to explore that possibility. Perhaps this is a source of stress to him.

My gf was urging me to give up on the illusion of this relationship, go out on dates to explore the endless terrain of possible alternatives. Im not hindered by a fear of being hurt again or a fear of being incapable of finding someone wonderful/capable of providing all those particular forms of care that are extolled as the height of a loving relationship. I simply want to pursue the possibility of this one and don't have a desire to be investing time and energy and value in others. I don't know if I'm living in a delusion. I have chosen to remain steadfast. Or as Hunter puts it, relentlessly stubborn.

*i also appreciate this opportunity to explore these topics w you - or as Hunter would describe it, deep dives aha x

11th October 2020

Deepika: Hellooooo this week has been crazy....I have 3 exams, my bf moved back to my city and my mom was threatening to kick me out (long story lmao) so it's been wild!!

Revenge is so complex and varied, I admire the subject! Anger, too. Especially female anger. Probably only female anger lol.

I also am guarded and inquisitive. I ask pointed questions to get a certain viewpoint through an answer (sometimes this isn't always good) so the concept is not unfamiliar to me.

And "the diced dick" sounds like so much fun to be a part of? I would sign up for that.

And my relationship has been a little much lately; he's great but almost too great. I feel like this is headed down such a serious path and I want it to be more casual and fun. He landed on Thursday and I went to see him at his new place and he asked me if I wanted a key - I don't even know what to say. And I think I was dissociating during sex with him bc of past s*xual trauma and idk....I really liked being alone. It's different to have him here in person. He really, really likes and loves me and I'm the first person to mean this much to him so I just feel...trapped? I think I like him bc I don't want to leave but other times im not so sure....do I just want to run away from this relationship bc I'm used to keeping people at a distance? Is it him or me? Uggghhhhg

Also, can I just say I admire your steadfast attitude in knowing what you want and standing by it! It's so mature and inspiring. I love that you have your own reasons for doing this and aren't trapped into cyclical thinking and using your thoughts to defend your actions

I'm so used to women going after and staying with shitty men for awful reasons. And I knoooow, I sound judgmental but it's only because these women are in my life and I have to hear about it. They don't stand by this man bc they want him and choose him (the way you choose Hunter—whether he's worthy of your time and attention is another matter ahah), they do it bc they're stuck in the situation. They're used to being in it so they choose it and defend it over and over. And they expect me to support them even though I don't agree with what they're doing....I'm never going to live people's lives for them so I'm not going to "call them out on it" either. I've been in similar situations with men that've deeply hurt me and my actions and inactions were a big part of it. women who can't establish themselves and set boundaries are really hard for me to be around. It reminds me of myself and I find myself empathizing a little too hard. That's why it's so refreshing to hear your view bc I didn't know people can be this strong and autonomous when it comes handling hurt, esp at others' hands

And how are things with Hunter btw? Is he upset about the zine and your depop??

13th October 2020

Margaret: Hey! Dam sounds like quite a lot is going on your end! I can def relate to the threat of being kicked out by mom (over the guy??). Bc that's exactly what went down for me in relation to Hunter.

My parents never approved of him from the start. They were particularly prejudiced against him for reasons that are by large beyond his control a) being white b) being American c)

being a bartender (and therefore must be a degenerate, drug using, no $$$$- just cast your imagination here for the nth degree of mom's worst nightmares and x1000 bc this is Asian mom w their unique brand of hangups and biases) c) they assumed he didn't go to University- O the Horror- and.... you get the picture. This was before they even met him- and they never have to this day.

It's an understatement to say that this is a source of conflict betw me and my parents. I am very protective of Hunter, and it has always hurt me to hear them pass judgement on him. I think it is unworthy of them.

Tbh I've never shared in their worldviews prior to this point in time, altho sometimes could see their logic. Yet I've never sought to make waves by defending my own viewpoints or indeed pursuing those differences.

I chose to flout it all to maintain a relationship with Hunter. And when I left Aus to go to Hunter during a moment of need, admittedly on v short notice (within 24 hrs of his request I flew from Syd to Boston), my parents were Furious, I was living w them at that time.

Three weeks later when I got back to Aus (I had secured approval from work and study it was all cool) I was immediately ejected- and I had to leave on the spot w my dog in tow. I stayed w a colleague while I looked for a place of my own. It was a particularly stressful period. And Hunter was Not supportive as he broke up with me pretty much as soon as I got back to Aus. But It was a difficult point in time for him then.

To cut a long story short, it's difficult but necessary to establish your own sense of independence from your parents.

Not in the sense of okay you're 18 out the door seeya at xmas or never ! and what's yours is yours mine is mine draw a line in the sand. But in the sense that you should develop your own sense of independence as a person, w your own integrity to pursue those things, to be content within your own identity. So that you know clearly what are your obligations that you are comfortable with. and you have the ability and means (and this may be financial) to make those critical decisions. I dunno, my parents in their infinite and unchallengeable wisdom would soundly disagree with that opinion.

As necessary and critical as it is to have familial support (example those families descended from generational wealth), I've always felt it is critical to establish your own means, to not be forced and under under some form of control.

But I suppose They would say that their control is nothing compared to the true control of the external society, an insidious control that robs you of even your awareness that your power and place is being divested from you. That their control is a means to help see beyond the distortion/mass mind pollution thrown up to keep the common masses downtrodden. To keep the family wealth and the unit, bc that's how families and wealth survive generations- a truth that society tries to rob its citizens of this awareness.

Yet I only want to be able to love the man I choose. And wish fervently that he would choose me in return. It is a selfish wish and pursuit. It doesn't grow familial wealth or expand through vaulting up the social ladders.

In how you describe your relationship atm.. Sometimes things get too serious too fast. I think that's part of what drew Hunter's reluctance toward me. I don't really understand it, bc I gues I've never felt this way. For me, it was only when I didn't feel like I had a real future w my partner (ie didn't love the dude) that I would rankle at his attempts to bridge the distance in intimacy. There's a chapter in Anne Carson, I had it on my depop not sure if it is still there: I wonder whether what you feel (and perhaps Hunter also) is something akin to what she describes here ^^

<Images from: Carson, A. (1986). Eros the Bittersweet: An Essay. Princeton, New Jersey; Guildford, Surrey: Princeton University Press. doi:10.2307/j.ctt7zv117>

There's a thrill to being desired, to the seduction that perhaps is lost when the relationship becomes more stable. I don't know, sometimes it's good to reflect on (although this may not be always clear) what it is you want. Firstly for yourself, and then in relation to this other person who's knocking on the doors of your life, asking to be let in. Sometimes these people are vandals, thieves, sometimes, they're snake oil salesmen. Sometimes they will knock for 99 days and then on the 100th day they will pack up and depart.

I don't know if I will depart. My temper is uncertain. I am fighting again w Hunter. Bc he failed to respond to me and when he finally did it was to say roughly that I had sent him too many msgs when he had failed to respond.

I told him I'm done with his mood swings after extending courtesy after courtesy. He met my challenge in saying to the effect he won't again msg me. In the past this would have made me rather despondent. But I am through with his bullshit. I shouldn't have to put up with this inconsistency, when I have put in all the effort to maintain this relationship while he barely rises to meet even a minimum.

But I also still love him. And am bound to honor that sentiment through actions and obligations if he is in need. I gues we just gotta cool it for a bit and try again later, again...

And.. I don't know whether like those women you describe, I'm using twisted logic to justify my desire to keep up with him, whether it is delusional, after all he did leave and we are apart. We al view our decisions a bit differently in hindsight.

It is probably and rightly viewed as crazy in that it is not a normal reaction or a standard decision to make, based on what is present- which is honestly not a lot. I can only choose what feels right to me, and do what I think is necessary in keeping with that.

18th October 2020

Deepika: It's not over my bf, they don't know he exists bc I haven't told them. I don't tell them anything about my life. I was going to spend Halloween weekend at my friend's place and my mom got angry and told me I was putting the entire family at risk and not to come back home and to leave. So I started looking for places to stay and my dad told me that she was bluffing and didn't actually want to kick me out lol. The entire situation is frankly ridiculous but they're both incompetent and ridiculous individuals so what could you expect, really. I don't think I have any love for my family, they're hard to love and not deserving. I'm stuck in this situation and can't leave bc I don't have the $$$$ to do so.

What your parents did sounds so harsh...is that why you became a dancer? To support yourself? (If you don't mind me asking).

I really don't mind being homeless because it's better than living with my family. It def won't be easy but I'm not worried for some reason.

I think my ambivalent attachment makes relationships painful. My longest relationships have been with my family and you can see the state of those lol so subconsciously I expect all relationships to be painful and difficult. The closer somebody gets, the harder it is. Other than my parents, my boyfriend is the only one who loves me and can do something about it. Realizing this made me cry but also helped me feel better. The relationship feels a lot better now than it did a week or so ago.

And I really don't think you're like the women I was talking about! They're not self-aware. One of them was my close friend and she literally told me she goes after horrible men "on purpose and she knows what she's doing."

(Those horrible men were a eugenicist, a fatphobic vet (she has an eating disorder) who moved drugs in the military and multiple fuckboys. Lol. She wanted me to be her yes-man and support and validate all these relationships with a "it's okay sis been there" bc I ALMOST got into a relationship with Xxxx, who was a white conservative. we stopped talking 6 months ago) .

It's good to hear that you're setting boundaries with Hunter. You seem like a wonderful partner with a lot to offer and you recognize your worth which is !! amazing. Idk, I may still have love for Xxxx, for some reason. It ended weirdly but I feel like he understood me on a deep, unspoken level. It's a shame it was unspoken but he never wanted to talk about problems or anything uncomfortable so c'est la vie...another reason the relationship had to end. He also reminded me a LOT of my parents, specifically the things I hated about them and how they would disrespect me. It just wasn't worth it anymore. My bf read the same piece I sent you (I showed it to him) and he said he felt bad for me bc I loved him a lot. My answer to that is: I mean, I guess? Idk enough to call it love. Maybe I did, maybe I didn't. But love can't take place by itself and I felt all alone when I was with Xxxx so that's a dead-end of a topic I guess.

19th October 2020
Deepika: have you heard of this? Xxxx and I have jung, I think.

<extract from a screenshot from Deepika, quote from Han, J. (2015). P.S. I still love you (First edition.). New York: Simon & Schuster BFYR>
There's a Korean word my grandma taught me. It's called jung. It's the connection between two people that can't be severed, even when love turns to hate. You still have those old feelings for them; you can't ever completely shake them loose of you; you will always have tenderness in your heart for them. I think this must be some part of what I feel for Genevieve. Jung is why I can't hate her. We're tied.

19th October 2020
Margaret: Hey :) was just about to write you. I'm not Korean, but I think jung *might?* be a version of the word jeong? The Korean word for love? But what that connotes is broader than the English/definition . Otherwise - it's the Korean version of this other Chinese concept concept 'Yuan'. I def believe in that idea tho.
   https://en.m.wikipedia.org/wiki/Yuanfen

19th October 2020
Deepika: That's fascinating to read, thank you.

19th October 2020
Margaret: Got called away to work sorry x and nice :) I've spoken to Hunter on the idea also, but yea I def believe in the idea of connections born of past, like energy that keeps repeating. There's a romance to it, this idea of being fated to unite out of the millions of possibilities, that it is in some way remarkable.

It's not some sort of doom that keeps repeating, but that there is something that can't be explained, a depth of connection. I think in translation the idea loses some of its metaphor. It's actually 2 words yuan and fen. Some people have the 'yuan' (the destiny and timing) but no 'fen' (the opportunity to develop to that outcome).

Sometimes a relation can be heavy in fen but no yuan, or vice versa. If you feel so, it is very likely that you have yuan with Xxxx. I believe without doubt that is my relation with Hunter. And that's already a uniqueness and something remarkable. But the fen... it's what holds us apart. I would give anything to realize this potential.

19th October 2020
Deepika: Can you actively deny fen? Like, walk away from it bc the person isn't good for you? Or does that count as no fen.

19th October 2020
Margaret: Aha that is the funny way of sayin it in Chinese. You got no yuan, or you got no fen. Lol. I think we create our own fen, but always within a context, and limited by that context. It's like opportunities; we recognize them and create them, but not in a vacuum.

You can walk away from someone because you won't allow that relationship to develop further, perhaps something about it is intolerable. That is a choice. We can choose and unchoose, to make our realities something that we can tolerate.

Just yea, in choosing or denying, do it for you, if it is right for you. And if it's unclear, give it some time. If it is yuanfen the opportunity will not simply evaporate. That's not to say no effort will cultivate a relationship, but I guess to try and take away the edge of urgency that sometimes can push us into hasty decisions/reactions.

And in responding to your msging earlier I try not to give relationship/personal advice either in support/critique bc I don't know the specificities to be casting my influence- I strongly believe in stepping back rather than dabbling under the guise of being helpful whether well-intentioned or not simply bc of the potential to cause more and unnecessary drama. It's not my call so I don't make it.

...I always want to encourage love where it is perceived as true, yet I always will abet calls to vengeance bc that's perhaps my true calling lol. But that said, I dunno, I don't want to be there making waves in relationships that I don't fully understand, or throwing my opinion when I don't indeed spend the time trying to comprehend the lived experience of another. I dunno, I think it's in some way irresponsible, and as consistent to this I also receive advice with a degree of distance.

The way you describe your relationship w your parents reminds me a lot of how I feel about my own. I love my parents, and I know they place full effort in trying to give me the best of every opportunity and to the best of their ability. But it is the difference in understanding what is best, what is right, and what is good in life- that difference in opinion and philosophy that drives us to conflict and division.

My parents will support me 100% in the pursuit of/the direction of what they believe is right. But they've never considered my thoughts, values, and time and time again have dismissed and lectured me extensively on the etc decadence and moral corruption of western (particularly American now that they are aware of my love for Hunter) values- that I have long given up on the possibility of an open discussion because I know that my words would fall on deaf ears and whatever I divulge would be used against me in various deliberate ways to curtail my freedom - this was when i was living with them as I was completing my masters and then later starting my PhD.

There is nothing more important than being independent. By that I don't mean to suggest to turn-against family (which always will have your best interests at heart, even if the ways they go about it are problematic/anachronistic). It is just so important to me, being able to establish the means to assert my own integrity as a person and to have the security in being able to do so. I just know too well what it feels like to be caged and to feel trapped.

Actually, I didn't take up as a dancer for the cash money aha. It was good $$$$ aha but I actually took up the audition on impulse to prove a point to a boy. Also named Xxxx.

I didn't know what to expect tbh from the experience, I just knew that it was wild, and a departure from what was normal and certain for me at the time. My identity at that time: I was fresh from high school, came from an academically-driven grade-competitive single-sex school; a freshman at art school, kinda just coming into my own, this ostensibly sensible Asian chick with glasses, n I dunno, I wanted to prove it to him?myself? that I could take and make it *whatever it was* into something that was my own.

It was an impulsive decision. I watched a demo of Courtney Love in the People vs Larry Flynt and my performance was based on that. I got the stint and continued to work it for a few months I think 6? My intention then grew to approach it as a form of journalism to write and document but also as a challenge to myself, and also as a reaction to Xxxx.

I was 19 and a virgin. I don't regret the experience (alas no more political career for me aha) but it was pretty grimy. This was why I urged Hunter not to go down this road, even if men and women have different experiences within the industry, I believe that it does rob you of a certain innocence. I don't want to think of him being hurt in this process, losing something essential through the harshness of that reality.

Try and leverage and build on what you have, to become stronger, to make a place for yourself in this world, that's kinda what I wanna do. Whether through your family or your relationships, these are all your strengths or limitations- depending on how well we manage the relation. You can only manage these relations effectively or share support w the ones you love when you are capable and strong yourself- strong enough to be able to afford to do so.

Having needed to extricate myself under dire conditions, I can def imagine that homelessness would be highly stressful and difficult to break from unassisted. I'm always trying I guess create options, so to avoid those situations that would be unhappily thrust upon me. Would be careful in building my capacity (financially/or otherwise) to create the security that I need.

Do you feel like it was love with Xxxx? Do you feel like it is love with your partner right now? Relationships are always changing. Length/duration is great on paper but it's in the commitment and what you bring to each other that's a more lived reality.

I've always looked for someone to understand me. I love Hunter because I feel that he does.

I was definitely in love with the first Xxxx (1.0), and another Xxxx (2.0) after that. And several other guys (enough w the Xxxx's aha). I don't want to go back and redact those memories and say nah it wasn't love bc I know better now what love is/could be. I felt strongly for those boys. I don't any longer. I also know it is not the same level/depth of connection/empathy as I feel for Hunter. Perhaps that is the yuan between me and Hunter.

As you described, it is something unshakeable. I get furious to the sky with Hunter. I would ordinarily have gone straight to vengeance and not looked back. I've only ever made concessions for him/because it is him.

But in relation to your gfs... I too have been w umm I guess questionable guys aha. I don't think they are horrible tho, or that I am specifically attracted to that 'horrible' quality- to me that feels a bit pointless... perhaps your gfs like the thrill of that uncertainty, of the drama in being w boys who are a little bit dangerous, less conventional, and something in a relationship that doesn't come by easily feels wilder, less tame and more exciting? I am only guessing here ;)

I never intro'ed Hunter as my bf to my parents. I don't tell my parents about my relationships. But I wanted to have him over for Xmas (this boy I met 2 weeks earlier) bc he's from the States and was a traveller, and was at a distance away from his actual family. However, my parents at last minute made a whiplash veto against the already agreed upon plan- citing drastic and unfounded prejudices- and so on Xmas day i instead drove to his and together we went on a car trip down south to the falls and beaches there. We spent Xmas together.

My parents didn't think that he was good enough for me. That idea made me feel horrible. I've listened to them Spout this type of nonsense judgement before but when they directed it at Hunter- I've never felt so viscerally- just sick to my stomach to my core. It wasn't bc I was in love w him even. I don't know. He wasn't my bf at that point in time. Just this strong sense that he didn't deserve this. I felt strongly protective of him, and I don't know, empathy over the rough experiences within his life, and I wanted to keep him from experiencing those moments if it was within my power. In recognizing the lengths that I would go, and I suppose the tenderness in those feelings, i realized relatively early on that I was in love with/love him.

I don't know at what point, maybe it was indeed earlier when I felt the connection with him; I can't describe it except to say that it is clear to me that I do love him, and thereupon followed all the corollary responsibilities as true to this idea.

For myself I find that all my relationships become a bit easier when i am in a more stable place (within and out). If you do recognize the patterns of behavior in yourself/or situations you may find yourself in, that might be more problematic (perhaps as in the ambivalent attachment style) - sometimes having the self-awareness/taking the time rather than reacting, to recognize those impulses/feelings that create the push/pull anxiety, is a step towards making those moments easier to handle.

What do you think it is that drew you or draws you to Xxxx? It's probably hard to give a summary bc it's not just certain qualities but the memories and shared experiences that make the relationship. Was it a single decisive choice in ending it? The idea of Jung/Yuanfen feels romantic and almost spiritual. Sometimes the opportunity is in the timing, the point you are both at in your lives. What happens when you keep someone in your heart? What happens when Yuan is met but Fen is not enough. How is that energy transformed or translated? Will it be another lifetime? And what do we do with those words entered into our poetic memory, as Kundera describes, the space which records all that charms or touches us, and makes our lives beautiful. Is it wishful thinking, perhaps an act of magical thinking, that I hope by keeping him within mine, somehow I too will remain in his, so that we may reconcile and reunite in the future? I hope for this fervently.

22nd October 2020

Margaret: <Screenshot, Take care of yourself, Sophie Calle> This is from Take Care of Yourself by Sophie Calle. her partner ended it w her abruptly by an email. She shared the letter to 107 women, professionals, and invited their interpretation/analysis. This compilation became her exhibition. This short story is part of the compilation x

23rd October 2020

Deepika: That's heartbreaking....thank you for sharing it with me.

You have really good taste in literature btw I want to go through your library!

I feel like these are good examples of what I felt towards Xxxx/the nature of our relationship.

<Screenshot 1 Sonnet 3, Sarah Tolmie; Screenshot 2 Lethe; Screenshot 3>

I guess learning about him was also learning about me...but it was painful to be with someone so callous and self-absorbed...what does that say about me....maybe I take things too personally? He did insinuate that I was the problem once.......

Maybe that's why I'm so investigative and love problem-solving.....if I solve problems then problems no longer exist and I am not a problem any longer...?

Also, a strong sense of ownership between us bc we knew each other intimately and I don't think anyone else knew him like that at the time.

It's definitely love with my boyfriend but a different sort of love than it was with Xxxx. And you're right—the opportunity simply didn't evaporate. Xxxx reached out to me a couple of times after we stopped talking but I couldn't get back into it, I just couldn't. Separating myself from him felt like peeling off my skin. I would cry for hours and hours over something that never was and it felt like I was mourning something meaningless, something I couldn't talk about, something I wasn't allowed to talk about because I was so ashamed to be in that situation in the first place.

Do you think caring for Hunter/feeling protective is what makes this relationship special? Or even simply having the opportunity to do so?

I don't want to introduce my bf to my parents anytime soon bc he's a different race from me as well and I don't want them keeping tabs on me and inquiring about my life and wondering if I'm having sex or going through my things....it's so much easier to pretend there's nothing going on as well (I'm Asian too, Indian to be specific).

The thing that made me angry about my friend is how much she lied about her life to me and expected me to validate her anyway. It's disrespectful but also unrealistic? She would be texting this guy and ranting about it on the phone with me about how much she hates him and how disgusting he is but when she sends me the screenshots she's blatantly flirting like....that's not what you said. Why are you lying? Why is it on me to deal with your issues? I couldn't believe anything that came out of her mouth.

<Screenshot from Deepika to Margaret: text from msg Margaret to Deepika>
I don't know at what point, maybe it was indeed earlier when I felt the connection with him; I can't describe it except to say that it is clear to me that I do love him, and thereupon followed all the corollary responsibilities as true to this idea.

Maybe this is all that love is. A duty. Maybe this is why people love, in the first place. This may be one of the clearest versions of love I've come across. Most versions are vague and irritatingly subjective.

23rd October 2020

Margaret: Do you feel that Xxxx holds qualities that you admire, or wish could be more developed in yourself? We all want to solve problems to a degree, curious to fix and to understand, but sometimes in haste and at our own pace rather than the pace of the other/world? That is my problem, often in my own relationships.

There is an aspect of duty and responsibility. You have a responsibility even in dreaming and imagination. Why not also in love?

Maybe as common sense suggests that in their absence you betray nothing and do nothing to alter the potential and that opportunity that at present at least doesn't exist in reality (it's a future hypothetical reality). That is very true and pragmatic in approach. Yet there's it feels to me- a sense of dishonor or denial of humanity that in some way takes place to use logic to justify that stream of reasoning.

You can use that brand of logic to justify away at everything until every action is distanced from a core emotivity and is a reasonable set of actions why not; you're here you're alive. I dunno, that's true and yea pragmatic, yet somehow distasteful.

It's strange how you describe the experience of enforcing the distance between yourself and Xxxx as like peeling skin. The very words I find myself using when I try to describe how it feels when im apart from H, when he enforces that upon me. There's something wholly excruciating in that distance, I find, in the inability to make those steps to close it, and in yearning for that outcome. It feels like this enduring suffering, unbearable and relentless.

I don't know whether I approach love the right way... for me it always opens/only opens after I make that choice to, tho perhaps it feels like there is no choice. The choice is to let them in (not inside your pussy- but your SOUL aha I'm kidding). But seriously. That connection/establishment has to be there for sure, but for it to progress to that level where I would describe it as love- with that idea of duty/responsibility in play- a conscious decision (one that I am legitimately aware of making) is required from me, to make that defined choice.

So while the feeling is real/authentic/all that- it isn't just a freefall- the element of responsibility is there bc that is how I enter/cross the threshold into love.

It's a heavy sort of love. Hunter struggled under its weight, and I also am not very paced, can be impatient and at many points lost my temper spectacularly. He endured much from me.

I don't know to take it seriously when another insinuates/apportions blame.... what Xxxx imputed of you. People may say it out of defensiveness or denial it's hard to face your own shortcomings esp when you can see that those limitations have hurt someone you care for. At least that's how I try to justify when Hunter loose cannons at me. I try not to take it personally bc it's only an outburst in the moment, under an emotional charge when he cannot handle it. I have moments like this too lol against him, I should hold it in bc he can't handle it when I get mad at him. I don't indeed believe it's ever all him or all me. Situations are always more nuanced.

Opportunities exists in that hypothetical realm, and live, so to speak, within the decisions you make towards or away from an intention, ofc negotiated with external forces. They exist for as long as you give life to their potential/remain open to the possibility. So basically, as long as you're around, the opportunity exists.

What you describe in making those hard choices, based on the reality of the qualities of your relationship w Xxxx, it takes a lot of resolution based on self-awareness and a firm handle of what is unacceptable/intolerable to you. ESP to keep with that decision firmly when indeed you still feel tenderness towards them. Is your decision irreversible? I know that when I make a decision to end a relationship, I do not allow myself to turn back. Over for me is over for ever.

In past relationships, when it was my call to end it, I was not sentimental or attached (hence my reason for ending it).

The only (perhaps) relationship? (tenuous) was a recent friend whom i have experienced intermittent moments of intimacy (emotional/physical) but um never made it past anything indeed perhaps bc I remained resolute on my ardent hope to reunite w Hunter, or bc he also didn't desire it? In any case it wasn't very clear. To I tried to be direct w him but perhaps was too callous in doing so.

I feel love for him, not the same or level of connection as w Hunter. Perhaps bc I didn't allow that possibility to grow/it was never there- who knows. It is with regret, but I felt I had to make my position clear- that I cannot be with him.

There is a sadness, when you recognize that relations come to an end/or have reached their run/will never be as close again from a point onwards/will drift apart by natural course.

The feeling of care/ protectiveness towards Hunter is definitely unique to this relationship, I've never felt this way inclined before. Not bc he's inept or needs protection. I think it's only one example of the feeling of tenderness, which I feel strongly in this relationship and never felt previously. I think in my interactions/friendships I'm more driven to give more, n not feel like I'm just taking-taking (in whatever sense). But that dynamic is always practiced w a reservation and distance, like almost so that they can make no claims over me or calls to guilt to control me.

I don't know what it is, but with Hunter I acted without that level of distance, and I was directly real? with him. I've never felt safe to with anyone, nor would again be so inclined to with another. I'm not sure whether this makes sense.

Did you also feel protective of Xxxx? Was the level of care for him something unique that contributes to elevate this relationship? Btw I asked my mother for her definition of yuanfen. She's a bit less romantic than me lol. She told me that it is opportunity to outcome x

***

Part four: Love

A reconciliation

28th August 2020

Pieces from letters/emails/text msgs/phone conversations
From: Margaret
To: Hunter

I began this Depop shop as a way to rid my life of everything tangible that reminded me of you and your actions. I set out with the intention of ridding myself of all the items that bore association with you; apparel that I had worn when we were together, or objects that you had left behind and had passed into my possession. I could not bear to come across these items in my daily life without thinking of you and feeling hard done by.

Always trying as an artist, I thought I could work with the concept of 'selling' heartache on the virtual realm of the Depop platform, as a sort of performance/conceptual artwork. The idea was to create a unique engagement with a collective audience of prospective buyers that I accrued through leveraging the market appeal of my designer label items for sale. I wanted to use the desirability of my items to reach a broader audience. In each listing, rather than focusing on providing a detailed description of the item for sale and constructing a narrative that would purposively promote the sale, I wanted instead to utilize the platform to address the collective buyers (the 'readership') in order to transmit my memories and reflections on our relationship.

In the character-limited space that was allocated to providing item descriptions for each listing, I narrated my sincere thoughts and recollections with the aim of exploring what it means to transmit memories as a transaction. I wanted to know what it meant to reach 'completion,' both as a performance/conceptual artwork, and also in knowing when/if I would finally be free from the heartache associated with your departure from my life.

At what time point and how would I know- for example at 100% sale of all items? Or perhaps when/if the memory saturation became dilute during the process, through continued consumption and engagement on the virtual global marketplace.

I didn't do this for the purpose of maligning you publicly. I have kept many details true to situations and have honestly described the emotions that I experienced
in response.

Below is the bulk of the textual exchange that has resulted from the body of work. Emotionally I am no longer in the same frame of mind as when I had set out on this venture. Unexpectedly, I have also made a friend with a girl in Houston- who knows if she and I may meet in the future.

I want to share with you the body of text, although I am not sure what I will do with it as yet. Perhaps nothing. As mentioned earlier, my account is Seralita and my password is XxxxxXX if you should ever care to look. It is curious, and I remain as ever.

Anyway x it is good to hear from you and to know you are alright. Let me know if you need anything at all.

Yours,
Margaret

29th August 2020

Text Msg
From: Hunter
To: Margaret
That's awesome, glad to hear it...and yea, thanks

29th August 2020

Text Msg
From: Margaret
To: Hunter
Thank you ☐ It's been unexpected the amount of response I've had from women msging me in relation to my item descriptions re you/heartbreak- I say this frankly. You're welcome to access my account in any case, I looked up my username Seralita (email: xxxxxxxxxx@gmail.com) and password is Xxxxxxxx

I wanted it as an honest capture n expression of what I experienced- rather than a soap-box to malign you- and I've tried to clarify this w those that have reached out

I dunno if you want anything that I've listed, they're mainly women's apparel, but yeah let me know I guess if you want anything changed/reworded/taken off. I dunno- if you got stuff that you don't want n maybe can sell off- maybe you could set up one yourself- it's free to list. If you want, I'm happy to list items for you on my account (which you've now got access) and can link all profits to your PayPal. x

Don't stress on the job. It sounds like an incredible experience even if it is in passing x

1st September 2020

Text Msg
From: Margaret
To: Hunter
Your birthday is approaching again as we enter September (21st as I recall). I don't know how you feel about it, but let me know if there is something you want/can do to make it special for you if it would bring you some happiness x

2nd September 2020

Email
From: Margaret
To: Hunter
Hunter, I sent you the draft text of the body of work developed thru my depop shop. Would you pls give a quick scan thru when you have time?

This is just an idea I was playing with...

It's still not the final version, I realize Iv still left out a few listings n need to adjust the dates/spacing, n may include a page/s of images. Intend to send you the final for a confirm when ready. I don't know yet what I want/can to do with it, but I'm keen to see it refined.

To answer the question I set out with: a piece is complete and heartbreak is resolved only when the artist/heartbreakee is at peace. In my case, thru engagement with others (world) and also with you (in the role of heartbreaker- sorry).

I also have the idea to give you space, opportunity and voice to critique and contribute your view (either directly onto the page in comment boxes where you choose, or as feedback to me to update the work). I don't know if you would be interested in doing so. Maybe not? But I've not done that before. Whatever you write I will not redact/alter. Credit to us both n commenters, happy to include names/protect privacy whichever you may choose.

If I end up monetizing it as an e-book or whatever (not sure I will/if it's worth reading- open to suggestions here) you're welcome to the full profits- and with full audience disclosure of the fact. This is because I want to create the same conflict in the audience/buyer of the tension and feelings of ambivalence that are present during breakups/n in selling items that once held/hold significance.

Format- I think it would be a 20-30 page document/booklet containing listings, comments from the audience, n if you are keen comments in the margins from you. I don't know how you feel about that?

Would u pls take some time to consider? I'll try n get the final version out (from me) in the coming days.

Yours,
Margaret

2nd September 2020

Email
From: Margaret
To: Hunter

FYI final body of text attached as word and pdf files (subject to editorial formatting – note that I will purposefully not make adjustments to grammar/spelling/content- only to visual/layout formatting) – will advise pictures if I end up producing them. Let me know… x

2nd September 2020

Email
From: Margaret
To: Hunter

Also, I hope you like the pun thrrr if you can see what I've tried to do.. x

2nd September 2020

Email
From: Margaret
To: Hunter
Hey sorry if it's been multiple emails today... just yeah im so incred. thrilled about putting it all together.

I think I'm okay with it as it is now.. as a literal catalogue. Please, it's not intended as devoted to slagging you off in entirety, I'm re-reading it myself and realize that it may appear this way, but please bear in mind that I began this at a point of high emotion, and the process does capture the evolution and reflection.

And I would obv totally get it if ultimately it's not up your alley um I just thought I'd ask. . I'm actually incred. anxious about your thoughts on it because I guess I still hold your judgement in esteem, and this is not something I've done before/and is unpolished and yeah personal. I hope you're okay with it at least, and if you're not, I won't release it publicly. And if you would like to be a part of the process, I would respect your comments/voice however much it may deviate from my own narration- and I wont redact/curate your text

I think a part of me is always obsessed with the idea of documenting/giving narration n therefore, mythology to valued experiences. In some way this^ has been an exercise in that n yeah I hope it's okay xx

3rd September 2020

Email
From: Hunter
To: Margaret
I think this whole concept is an awesome idea, and outlet for you. Not only is it creative, but expressive, therapeutic, and you get to clean out your closet a bit and make some money. I don't feel comfortable editing this though and I hope you understand why. I have read it though. Keep doing you and doing art, and being creative. My birthday is coming and maybe I got my eye on a Giles and Brother piece ;)...

I'm glad you're doing well...

Take care

3rd September 2020

Email
From: Margaret
To: Hunter
Thanks Hunter x I'm really glad you're not averse to the concept and my writing. I was nervous. Your opinion matters a lot to me. I tried to keep the writing quite tight n true (each listing also had a character limit) and yeah it was an oddly public and consumerist experience- having ppl 'liking' commenting and msging n buying. I might still play around w formatting n the idea of distribution and see what I can/want to do with it, whether or not to add an afterword section. If it gets to some stage I'll send you either a physical or digital copy. If it becomes something, happy to divert all proceeds to you. I really like the idea of posing that discomfort in the buyer (not that I think ppl are just swarming to buy my random writing).

The shop/concept/performance piece is complete- I mean there are still listings but yea it's just a feeling, like when you're painting or drawing or even writing- somehow you just Know when a piece is done. It wasn't what I had set out to achieve. I wasn't looking for solidarity and I firmly don't believe in 'female solidarity/sisterhood' - which i don't want this be read as a promotion of. I'm more interested in the documenting, interpretation and transmission of memories.

For your bday if you like, I'd be more than happy to get the G&B item for you x send me a link to the page? Can have it shipped to you - do you have a home/work address? Otherwise, happy to direct it to your mother x

3rd September 2020

Email
From: Margaret
To: Hunter
Ps sorry for being a paean in the ass ahaha

4th September 2020

Text Msg
From: Margaret
To: Hunter
Let me know re the G&B x n just FYI to note that there may be some delay to international shipping cos of covid, even w express post ps picked these up from the antique store the other day, I think they're incredible x

5th September 2020

Text Msg
From: Hunter
To: Margaret
What did you get?

> https://www.gilesandbrother.com/products/embedded-dagger-necklace

Was kinda looking at this either gold /silver...

My address is...
xxx Xxxxxx Xxxx
Xx Xxxxxxxx, Xxxxxxxx XXXX
(XX)

I'm still kinda looking but, yea i wanted to treat myself to one of G and B pieces for bday,,, after this factory life

I think ill stay here for another month or so then I'll go somewhere else

> https://www.gilesandbrother.com/products/id-bar-stripe-wrap-rope-cuff

>https://www.gilesandbrother.com/products/leather-wide-visor-cuff

I dno these are kinda cool too but the necklace is sweet what you think? Thanks again for help with setting up frontiers acct... Let me know how your depop shop goes! I think honestly its a clever idea again, like as an art form/creative piece/while still being entrepreneurial..

5th September 2020

Text Msg
From: Margaret
To: Hunter
I like the bracelets :) but the necklace!! It's sick n I'm drawn to the gold finish over the silver hbu? Ill shoot the shop a note to ask what their estimates are for international express post to NZ and what company they can go with (USPS or DHL- I've had good experience w DHL express during the covid). Let me know when you decide, I'm happy to place the order.

I got the turquoise foo dogs (stone lions actually)! They're meant to protect your abode but got them mainly for the color n the close resemblance they bear to pugs.

The shop has been a great way of exchange (items and communication) w other women. Still msging this girl in Houston who act shared her own writing w me. It's been an odd but valuable experience. Not loving posing redacted selfies to demo clothing fit tho. It's not a talent I possess apparently

5th September 2020

Text Msg
From: Hunter
To: Margaret
Yea I like the gold one, was first choice for sure

Oh I see, yea nice... That's funny you're meeting others through it. Aha and yea do some selfies who cares

5th September 2020

Text Msg
From: Margaret
To: Hunter
Sweet x I'll see what they write back on the postage options (check whether they can do express post w anticipation to arrive by your bday). If it's all good, I'll make the buy n share tracking etc

Ahaha do you think the porcelain dogs are hideous

And yeah i know it's strange how connections are made.

29th September 2020

Msg on Whatsapp
From: Hunter
To: Margaret
Sorry I'm super busy/stressed at the moment with my own things. This is your art/project and I think you should continue on with it. However, I don't feel comfortable or want to be a part of it. I will read it when you finish, but this is your thing. Not mine. I have so much going on just do it but you don't need my advice, and honestly I feel uncomfortable about it, and you asking me. I hope you understand.

30th September 2020

Email
From: Margaret
To: Hunter
I'm sorry for stressing you earlier. I don't know- I speculate that you're still raw on me contacting you/telling you the words I love you? I can't recall if I said this, but perhaps I said something consistent with that meaning in effect.

It's been an introspective process for me, to refine what I want this text to tell, and what impact I want to make with it. I've spoken to very many people; professionals, friends, colleagues, strangers passing through, etc. I've done a lot of delving into past conversations, including saved chat logs between you and I (I had done a complete backup-download of my history of msger conversations at some point before I permanently deleted my FB account and all the information associated with it), and found a msg from me to you:

FB Msger
Hunter: You offer me support
Feb 12, 2019, 2:15 PM

Margaret: Whatever choices you make (come here/stay there/do this/be with whomever) I want to support you, and freely because I really want you to be happy
Feb 12, 2019, 2:16 PM

On reflection, I don't think I have changed. But perhaps you have bc you are the one who left, and you're more open to this. But I stayed, I am more fixed, and I'll remain, regardless of the outcome whether it is conventional, glad, or tragic.

I don't want to stress you, I don't want you to be unhappy bc of me. I will go offline now. But I remain always here for you.

Yours,
Margaret

A retrospective

9th April 2019

Email
From: Hunter
To: Margaret

TheWeather

Today it rained...

It was only after I read your note, when I realized that the overcast clouds had fallen low, and with them settled a steady, heavy, cleansing rain. l couldn't help but feel an unmistakable air of melancholy that this type of weather brings about, despite the fact that my morning began in relatively high spirits. This type of weather does inspire me with deep thoughts, reflections, and makes me ponder the state and nature of things/subjects ranging far and wide... Do you like the rain?...I think I already know the answer...

You wanted a bit of a letter and, well, here I am entertaining your request. You do write very well, I can't help but see/read a little Plath/poet in you...and in a sentence where you ascertain you don't use poetic prose, you follow it with talks of the "mire of daily life....diving into pools...with scintillating clarity of mud...etc." Although poetic, and the usage of metaphor, both gravitating and clever, I can't help but feel that sometimes it all comes across as ostentatious, and you are trying too hard to prove your validity as a writer. This, by the way, is what I'm attempting-feebly-to do now. Not that I think you are, particularly like that, but this is again- I feel -a tool and means (to write to me in correspondence) to practice your dialectic, and skills with the pen (and keys), which I know you enjoy. Your writing I find is overall sad in nature which then makes me sad thereafter reading it. It's like you're a caged bird, desperately seeking a means of communication, singing, in an empty room, looking-searching for an outlet of expression, which you have thus far kept bottled up and internalized...

At least you do still sing...I am, in no way, trying to put you down, it's just sometimes I feel bad after reading this- some of the things you write. I see gray... You do realize,

that this isn't the "normal" prose that people take when trying to an express an idea on a particular matter, don't you? After reading a seven paragraph letter, explaining the undertakings of a day, or a few fleeting thoughts, that all could have been expressed with equivalent clarity in 5-10 sentences I can't help but wonder why? Why the need for the superfluous nature of it all? Do you sit back, and admire, quite satisfied by your own eloquence??
But I think I know why..It's just..Sometimes it's all so heavy, too heavy, for me to bear.

I suppose it's better than being unbearably light? ;)

Keep writing tiger..
Hunter

Sometime, mid-late 2019
Date uncertain

Msg
From: Margaret
To: Hunter

Please.
Ready leaf on the loose branch,
A green pearl in my hand,
Too unripe to thread but precious
All the same and I cannot let go
Or bear to see it roll from my
Palm or be held in the palms of
Others.
Ready though you may be but
You are not and nor am I
Prepared to see you depart from me,
To imagine a life without,
as I could not bear
to be prepared to be ready,
Though you may be, and I ask
Are you?
Ready yourself and I will too,
Strip myself to bear it and be
Torn off this tree while I am unready,
Bare and green as I am ripped
To be kneaded and moulded and
Placed on display before all to be
Threaded.
A hole runs through me; I think I am
Now ready to bare my skin before
You when you tell me though I was
Always bare before you, but now I
Am ready to bear this once more,
To be threaded through this hole-
I am ready.
Line my pockets I am ready to
Patch the holes that would release
Me from the bottom and weight the
Wait with tension but be steady as
I was born ready to count my breath
And release it in one sigh to glimpse
The surface and sink with purpose
To be.

Or not to be ready and peer over
The yellow and count the teeth and
Look for bright eyes in the dark shining,
Only to be reminded of a gaze always
Fixed on me and be pulled back
To the surface from a violence that is
Not to be. Yet.
Fill up this hole and I will be ready for
A lifetime within a breath to be
Released and contained by these
Branches of a forest overgrown and
Unlit but for the moon above
glowing like the eye of my hound
Alongside me, ready to tear apart all who
Trespass.
This silence is heavy, but I am ready
To be still whether above or below
The surface of this reflection though
I cast none and can no longer tell
The difference between night and day
Since you never dared to stay to make me
Tremble.

?   <Fini>

Acknowledgements

Thank you to:

Deepika, Hunter, NausicaaNoor, and those on Depop who shared their comments, views, and support.

Hunter for always being my light of inspiration.

Kang, Fan, for your support in picking me up from down under.

And to my **Gran** who rode with me and stood by me the entire way.

I love you.

Text, images & editorial by Seralita

Much love to you all xo

www.ingramcontent.com/pod-product-compliance
Lightning Source LLC
Chambersburg PA
CBHW061327040426
42444CB00011B/2804